Specter's

What Not to Do

Italy

A Unique Travel Guide

Plan your travel with expert advice and Insider Tips: Travel
confidently, Avoid Common Mistakes, and indulge in Art, Culture,
History, Food, and nature.

Sarah Brekenridge

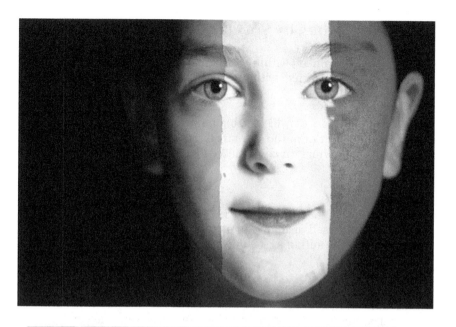

Table of Contents

Introduction

In Italy, they add work and life to food and wine. –Robin Leach

A h, Italy. Home to some of the most extraordinary landscapes, like the rivers and gondolas in Venice and the Leaning Tower of Pisa. Italy's country has many gorgeous colors around the cities and towns, ancient buildings, and landscapes that enchant even the most seasoned traveler. And don't forget the delicious food and the love and work that goes into creating the many tasty dishes. There is so much to do, see, and experience in Italy; it can feel overwhelming when you never have been and have no idea where to start. But it shouldn't be! Traveling to such a beautiful country with rich history and cuisine should be thrilling!

I traveled to Italy in 2019 and was amazed to roam around Italy. One of the first

things I appreciated early on was how culturally diverse the country is. A one or two-week itinerary won't be enough to experience the various diverse areas of Italy, especially if you've never been before. However, visiting classic destinations such as Milan, Cinque Terre, Venice, Tuscany, Rome, Naples, Pompeii, the Amalfi

Coast, Sicily, and the Italian Lake District might be on your list. We'll be going through the dos and don'ts for these destinations so you can plan your trip accordingly to see at least one or two of these regions. While traveling to Italy, I realized that there are many things one should keep in mind to avoid common pitfalls that may adversely impact the travel experience. In writing this travel guide, I aim to highlight the 'To Do" list in Italy and make you aware of things you should 'Not Do' in Italy.

Food is the soul of Italy. As for the delicious food in Italy, we don't need much of an introduction. Italian food is well-loved among everyone, but it's the love and

passion that goes into making their dishes and gelato! I have seen the love and care that goes into making pasta and pizza. Food and feeding people are arguably the most prominent love language all Italians share. On your trip, you will get the chance to experience this, and I will guide you to some of the best little places to check out!

Italy has some impressive art and architecture. While Florence has a significant artistic heritage, Rome, Venice, and Verona also stand out with their art and landmarks. You'll never fall short of masterpieces to see! While artists such as Michelangelo and Donatello are a couple of the first names that come to mind when you think of art, by traveling to other regions within Italy, you may discover a love for some artistic underdogs and find an appreciation for other sculptures, churches, and palaces that make up Italy.

Many don't realize that before Italy became a unified country, it had various regions and kingdoms, such as the small nations within the country. Because of this, it creates such a fascinating history because they each have a different past. If you are a history buff, you won't fall short of learning more about how areas like Rome can teach you about its ancient empire and how you can experience and learn more about Italy's Middle Ages and Renaissance period in Florence.

But if there is one thing that anybody can appreciate about Italy, aside from its rich history and culture, it is the people that live there. They are sometimes loud, obsessed with food, and outgoing! Chances are (depending on where you stay and visit), you'll leave Italy with some newfound friends.

All of these beautiful ideas aside, I can understand that if you travel once every couple of years, have never traveled in your lifetime, or have never been to a foreign country, it can feel overwhelming. Even a seasoned traveler can find planning to be daunting at times. But I am here to tell you that planning your trip to Italy can be manageable. In this book, you won't need to sift through excessive information on what you should and shouldn't do in Italy. I will give you the necessary information to help you plan your trip effectively and efficiently so you can stop stressing about what way to use "Ciao" and enjoy your trip.

As for the landmarks, there is no way you'll see them all in one trip! That's okay! While there are many iconic attractions, please don't feel you need to cram them all in. Not only will it leave you feeling exhausted and stressed out, but it will also take away the enjoyment of your trip. You can immerse yourself in many pieces of culture, history, and art in a balanced way to savor the moments and memories!

Lastly, one of the biggest concerns of traveling is how to budget, culturally adapt, and remain safe while traveling. With an overflow of information, it's natural for anyone to feel confused about navigating these areas of concern, but that's what you have me for!

In this book, we will look at all the ways to plan your trip to Italy so that you have one of the (many) best trips of your life! We'll first discuss the best time to go to Italy (because every country has its high tourist time versus something quieter), what essentials you need to know for booking, and much more that goes into planning your trip.

Once we go through the planning hacks, we'll explore the tips and tricks for Italy, such as navigating their transportation system, being respectful and following cultural etiquette, and other mistakes to avoid when traveling in Italy.

In the meatballs and pasta of the book, we'll look at a bunch of different cities you may be considering on your trip and the dos and don'ts for each.

From this book, please take away that planning your trip to Italy does not need to be overwhelming and stressful! You should be able to plan a fantastic trip with my hacks and travel knowledge. As an old Italian proverb says, *Chi non va non vede, chi non vede non sa e chi non sa se lo prende sempre in culo.* (Translation: Those who don't go don't see, those who don't see don't know, and those who don't always take it in the ass.) You won't see everything the first time, but hopefully, your first trip will be the trip that makes you want to return so you can see more of this beautiful country.

Chapter 1

Planning Your Trip to Italy

I n Italy, the phrase "la dolce vita" is a way of life, meaning to live a sweet and fulfilling existence. Italians are known for their pride, enthusiasm, and strong connections with family and friends. They value each day as a gift and celebrate it with their love for food. To fully appreciate their culture, it's best to embrace their way of living and take each day without worrying about trivial

things. By doing so, planning your trip to Italy will become easier and more enjoyable.

Beautiful Italy

Let's be honest: it was rough when we couldn't travel for a few years due to the pandemic! We had to rely on technology to take us to other countries! However, with the ability to travel again, many want to take those online excursions offline and begin exploring international destinations.

Italy is a popular country to visit thanks to its vibrant attractions, fascinating heritage, and mouthwatering cuisine. Despite its unique shape on maps, Italy offers many breathtaking locations, each providing a unique cultural experience. This southern European country comprises a vast peninsula and two islands, Sardinia and Sicily, in the Mediterranean Sea. Italy shares its borders with France, Austria, Switzerland, and Slovenia, with the majestic Alps running along the northern edge.

The roots of Italian society and regions can be traced back to around 1200 B.C.E. Since then, Italy has seen the rise of the Roman Empire and the Renaissance period, beginning in the 15th century, dramatically influencing culture, architecture, and Italian art, inspiring many globally. Tourists visit the numerous basilicas, cathedrals, arenas, forums, and piazzas, delving into the country's rich history.

I love how Italy was once a collection of small states and regions, and the country now offers an abundance of diverse environments for travelers to explore, particularly those seeking the perfect vacation spot. If bustling cities are your thing, you can't miss Rome. On the other hand, if you're looking for a tranquil retreat, the Italian Lake District is the perfect destination. And we can't forget the gorgeous landscapes of wineries and their history as you drive through the countryside! While I have traveled a lot, thinking back to the view takes my breath away. It was out of this world for me to see the rows of grape vines and learn how the vineyards came to be.

Italy is breathtaking, and while we are only getting started on planning your trip, I know your experience will be memorable and unique to you. But first, when is the right time to go?

Planning your trip to Italy

The most crucial decision in planning your trip is to decide which locations to visit based on how many days you plan to spend in Italy. Ideally, you should set aside three weeks for your visit, but I understand that not everybody can spare three weeks. Hence, I have come up with recommendations for one-, two- and three-week itineraries for Italy travel. My recommended itineraries will give you some ideas on how to plan, but I would also suggest making changes as per your interests. If you like art and history, you should spend more time in Rome and Florence. For shopping and leisure, Milan and Venice are the best places. If you are interested in mountains and nature, plan more

days in the Lake District and Dolomites. Soaking in the sun is your priority, then Cinque Terre and Amalfi Coast are the best bets.

One-week itinerary

Day	Plan	Stay
1	Arrive at Rome	Rome
2	Rome	Rome
3	Rome	Rome
4	Rome to Florence	Florence
5	Florence	Florence
6	Florence	Florence
7	Florence to Venice	Venice
8	Venice	Venice
9	Depart from Venice	

Two-week itinerary

Day	Plan	Stay
1	Arrive at Rome	Rome
2	Rome	Rome
3	Rome	Rome
4	Rome to Naples	Naples
5	Naples to Amalfi	Amalfi
6	Amalfi	Amalfi
7	Amalfi to Naples to Florence	Florence
8	Florence	Florence
9	Florence	Florence
10	Florence to Milan	Milan
11	Milan	Milan
12	Milan to Venice	Venice
13	Venice	Venice
14	Depart from Venice	

Three-week itinerary

Day	Plan	Stay
1	Arrive at Milan	Milan
2	Milan	Milan
3	Milan	Milan
4	Milan to Cinque Terre	Cinque Terre
5	Cinque Terre	Cinque Terre
6	Cinque Terre	Cinque Terre
7	Cinque Terre to Rome	Rome
8	Rome	Rome
9	Rome	Rome
10	Rome	Rome
11	Rome to Naples	Naples
12	Naples	Naples
13	Naples to Amalfi	Amalfi
14	Amalfi	Amalfi
15	Amalfi to Naples to Florence	Florence
16	Florence	Florence
17	Florence	Florence
18	Florence to Venice	Venice
19	Venice	Venice
20	Venice	Venice
21	Depart from Venice	

The Best Time to Go to Italy

No matter when you plan to travel, it will always feel a bit hectic because you're leaving the comfort of your home to embark on an adventure. Of course, when planning a trip to somewhere like Italy, you'll want to consider the right time for you. Are you someone who loves warmer or hot temperatures or cooler weather?

Italy experiences all four seasons, but each has benefits and downfalls. Additionally, the various regions have differing conditions and temperatures. For example, if you are going to the southern part of Italy in the summer, it could be scorching compared to the northern part of the country, which may feel significantly cooler. Therefore, depending on where in the country you intend to visit, the seasons and climate will implement how you plan your trip to include your specific interests and preferences.

Climates and Seasons

Spring in Italy is between March and May. You can expect the weather to be relatively mild and pleasant during the day but cooler in the evening. During the day, you can expect temperatures to range between 55.4°F and 62.6°F. However, these temperatures will differ based on the region you visit. Going to Italy in the spring is an excellent time because it's not tourist season yet, so the lines to get into attractions won't be as long or busy. The bonus is that airfare is also a bit cheaper during these months!

Spring is also an excellent time to check out some festivals, such as the Almond Blossom Festival, which began in 1936 in Agrigento, Sicily. This fun festival was once a harvest festival but has since expanded into an international event with various performances with folk groups. It's super neat! If you want to check it out, the Almond Blossom Festival takes place around the end of February or early March, depending on when the blossoms begin.

If the summer months are more your cup of tea, summer in Italy is between June and August. This is a great time to go if you are a beach lover and want to take advantage of the sun! You can expect temperatures to range between 71.6°F and 104°F. If that's not hot enough, some people love to check out the hot springs in Tuscany to try out their healing properties! If this is the time you want to go, pack some light clothes (and don't forget the swimsuit)!

I know not everyone loves the hot weather, so autumn may be a better time for you to walk around the cities without feeling like a melting gelato. Autumn in Italy brings some balanced temperatures: it's not too hot or cold, it's just right! Autumn in Italy is between September and November, and you can expect to take some stunning photos with the leaves changing colors or falling off the trees! If you want to check out some wineries, this is the time when they harvest their grapes to make wine. Some tours may even let you try the old-fashioned way of stomping on grapes and then enjoying a glass or bottle of wine.

Verona is another popular area to visit in the fall, as every September 12, people commemorate the death of Shakespeare's Romeo and Juliet. If you plan to visit Italy in the fall, expect temperatures between 46°F and 82°F.

Winter in Italy begins in December and lasts until February. It varies across the country. In the northern part, you can expect more snow and the chance to ski or snowboard in the Italian Alps. Outside the northern regions, snow doesn't typically accumulate on the ground. You can check out some lovely Christmas markets in December and enjoy the charming Christmas Italian cheer! Book early if you want to ski because ski resorts tend to get busy. As for temperatures, expect temperatures to be between 23°F and 55.4°F.

You will also want to keep in mind that while Italy has a range of temperatures, they will differ depending on whether you are in the northern or southern part of the country. Those temperatures can change dramatically between the regions, especially in the winter. If you are going to Northern Italy, have some sweaters on hand, especially when there is a chance of snow. As for the southern region, summer is hot, but the temperatures cool off in the evening, so you will want to have a light sweater on hand. When packing, check the weather about a week before your departure so you can pack your clothing accordingly.

Peak Tourist Season

Peak season in Italy is one of the more popular times, especially for families with kids. If you plan a trip to Italy between June and August, be prepared for the attractions and sites to be busy! However, the summer is also a peak time for festivals around the country. Some of the famous festivals include

La Notte Biana (The White Night): This festival happens in Rome and involves a night of dancing and music. Some museums and other cultural institutions tend to stay open later, too!

La Festa del Redentore (The Feast of the Redeemer): This traditional festival happens in Venice to honor the Redeemer, the city's patron saint. As Venice is well known for its rivers and gondolas, watch a procession along the Grand Canal in addition to fireworks!

Il Festival delle Sagre: If you love good Italian food, this is one festival for you! Sagre food festivals happen in various cities around Italy to celebrate hunting or harvest seasons. When these festivals take place, they often occur between June and August.

Off-Peak Season

If busy seasons are not your thing, consider planning your trip to Italy in its less busy season between November and March. With fewer tourists, it means you are not waiting in long lines, and your hotel and airfare prices are lower. Plus, it is less hot depending on where in the region you are.

April to mid-June and September to October are the shoulder seasons to visit Italy. In those months, you have the best of both worlds as the weather is comfortable, and again, you won't face the same crowds as you would from July until August or early September. This means you can take some pleasant strolls and see the trees and flowers start to bloom in the spring or enjoy the harvest time in the fall, all without the craziness of extra tourists flocking to the same areas as you.

Special Interests

What does your dream Italian vacation look like? Do you envision seeing the historical attractions in Rome, or do you want to drive through Tuscany's countryside to visit the various vineyards? Where you want to go will all come down to what interests you. However, remember that the seasons (both weather and tourist) and your budget also will impact your plans.

Wine Tours

If you plan to visit some wineries in Italy, your best bet is to explore the wine regions in the early spring or fall. However, if you want to partake in the harvest festivities, your best bet is to go in September or October.

Hiking and Winter Sports in the Dolomites

The Dolomites is a stunning area in Northeastern Italy and worth visiting in any season. Depending on your interests, you should plan your winter trip to the Dolomites if you enjoy winter sports; otherwise, spring, summer, and fall are excellent seasons for hiking and taking in mountain views.

Art Galleries, Museums, and Historical Landmarks

Going to Italy's art galleries, museums, and other historical landmarks is good in any season. However, it's even better during the shoulder and off-peak seasons because you'll spend less time waiting in queues. If you plan a trip to Italy in those slower months, being inside to take in history, art, and culture isn't bad during these seasons—especially if it is cooler and wetter outdoors.

Booking Essentials

Booking any trip can feel overwhelming, especially if you are unsure what needs to be booked in advance. Having some ideas on where to start is helpful, but you still want some wiggle room for your trip. While planning your trip to Italy, be mindful of your timing and the month (or months) you intend to be in Italy, especially when booking your flights and accommodations!

Flights

Forty airports throughout Italy offer various domestic, international, and intercontinental flight connections. If you're coming from the United States, you will likely want to fly to one of the following airports (depending on where you want to start your holiday):

- Milan Malpensa Airport (MXP)
- Venice Airport (VCE)
- Rome Airport Fiumicino (FCO)

- Naples Airport (NAP)
- Lamezia Terme International Airport (SUF)
- Bologna Guglielmo Marconi Airport (BLQ)
- Bergamo Orio al Serio International Airport (BGY)

When you go to book your flights, be mindful of where you want to land in the country. From there, it's a matter of how close you want to be to the city center.

That said, I also recognize that when it comes to budget, everyone wants to find a flight that won't break the bank. Remember that your trip to Italy during the off-season will be a little cheaper, but if you intend to bask in the sun for some of those days, going during the off-season likely will not allow you to enjoy this activity.

Regardless of which season you plan to go, it's unfortunately not as simple as plugging in the dates you wish to travel to buy your flight tickets at a reasonable rate—it takes some strategy. Some standard techniques we might have previously known and used to book flights are outdated. Here are some common mistakes travelers make when booking their plane tickets.

Booking the Cheapest Fare

Sure, United, American, and Delta Airlines have basic fares if you want to sit in the economy section. Still, the downside to their cheapest fares is that they don't allow you to bring a carry-on without a fee, let alone the ability to decide which seat you want or if you need to change your ticket. That's not ideal, especially when you'll be on the plane for at least seven hours! Ideally, if the budget permits, you should book an economy seat with more leg space for flights over six hours. It's absolutely worth it for a comfortable journey.

The fares are enticing, but expect to pay more out of pocket for other things, such as your carry-on and seat selection. At that rate, you're better off paying the full economy fare upfront instead of paying extra for the perks after the fact!

Booking Too Early or Too Late

If you have ever booked your flights late, you know how costly it can be. However, the same rule applies even if you book them too early!

For Italy (and any international country), I suggest booking flights between three to six months before you'd like to arrive. If you want to monitor flight fares to ensure you don't miss a fare drop, apps like Kayak, Hopper, and Google Flights can track the flights you are looking for and let you know when it's time to book.

Buying Flight Tickets on the Weekend

Most everything has an algorithm, and the same goes for buying plane tickets. More people tend to buy domestic and international plane tickets over the weekend. As flight companies expect this, there are fewer deals to take advantage of. Instead of booking your ticket on the weekend, set an alert using one (or all) of the apps I mentioned earlier.

Not Being Flexible in Travel Plans

Are the dates you want to go to Italy firm, or are you willing to have some wiggle room? Regarding airlines, most booking systems can let you put dates on either side of the days you want to fly. Some days before or after your intended departure date might be cheaper.

Not Flying Mid-Week

Most people like to fly to destinations on Mondays, Fridays, and weekends, making them the busiest days! Consider flying mid-week instead. You may even find some deals by flying between Tuesday and Thursday.

The same rule applies to booking hotels for your trip. Booking your hotel on a weekday is sometimes cheaper than on the weekend.

Accommodations

Once you book your flight, the next question you may wonder is where the best place is to stay while on your trip. Plenty of accommodations are available from hotels, hostels, vacation homes, farm stays, and bed and breakfasts, but knowing which is the better option for you might be daunting.

One of the first things you should be looking at is where the accommodation is on the map. For example, if you opt to stay at a hotel in Rome and it is marketing itself as such, make sure it's in the city and not outside, especially if you plan to use transportation instead of renting a car. That said, if you are planning to stay at a hotel, it's good to double-check and see if breakfast is included in the rate. Even if it is, checking the most recent reviews will tell you what those breakfasts are like. Other things to remember when looking at accommodations are

- ensuring taxes are included with your room rate.
- paying attention to how many people can stay in a hotel room.

A note about the room limits: Room limits are set by the law, so if you have more people than the allotted number it sleeps, hotel managers cannot accommodate the additional heads. However, before booking, ask if the hotel can bring an extra bed or two into your room for an additional fee, as most hotels can allow two people and an additional bed if you are a family of four to six people. However, at that point, I suggest booking an apartment.

- Find out if the rate is per person or per room.
- Ask about parking if you are renting a car, as not all hotels have free parking or any parking for that matter.
- Checking flight arrival time with the hotel check-in time. If your flight arrives early in the morning and your check-in is at noon, it's better to check with the hotel to see if they will allow early check-in and what the additional charges are. However, if possible, avoid early arriving flights to avoid the extra charge of checking in early.

Activities and Tours

Book tickets in advance when planning to see the more popular attractions, especially if you are going during peak season! Otherwise, you may end up standing for hours in a long line only to find out that the tickets for that day are sold out. The same rule applies to other activities, such as classes or short tours. Aim to book these activities about three months in advance. Otherwise, these schedules are released approximately six weeks ahead of other events, such as festivals or performances.

When you consider the things you'd like to do in Italy, you still want to keep in mind where in proximity your accommodation is and how you'll get to it!

That said, there is a lot to see and do in Italy, so if you want to book a tour, here are some of the top suggestions:

Rome Free Walking Tour: This is a perfect tour to join, and it's free! This group offers several free tours daily that you can adapt to your trip and what interests you. The tours last around two hours.

Italy Food Tours: If you are a foodie, this tour is for you, my friend! Even if you aren't someone who lives by trying different foods, you can't go wrong on a tour with Italy Food Tours. Italy Food Tours is highly rated by National Geographic, Forbes, and Lonely Planet because they dive into the many Italian cuisines! They will take you on food and drink tours, and if you want to try making an authentic Italian dish, you can take a pasta-making class. Italy Food Tours runs tours in Rome and Florence and are about three to four hours long.

Strawberry Tours: To go beyond the free walking tours in Rome, look at Strawberry Tours. These guys will work alongside other companies that run tours in Rome, Milan, Florence, and Venice to get an overview of each city with the local expert guides. These tours typically run for two to three hours but go more in-depth. In addition, Strawberry Tours offers paid tours if you want something unique. Depending on the tour, these paid ones start at around 30 euros per person.

Visa Requirements and Necessary Documentation

According to the Italian Embassy (n.d.), if you are a citizen of the US or Canada, you do not need any visa to travel to Italy, provided you are not spending more than 90 days in Italy. The US, Canada, and Schengen Area have visa-free arrangements. But you should ensure your passport is valid until at least three months after your planned return home.

It is worth noting that from 2021, US citizens will need to apply for an 'ETIAS visa waiver' before they travel, which can be obtained online and will cost €7 ($7.82).

U.S. residents and green card holders who are not citizens and hold a passport from a state without a visa-free travel agreement with the Schengen Area should apply for a Schengen Visa via the nearest Italian consulate.

US citizens planning to stay in Italy for over three months must obtain an entrance visa from an Italian consulate before coming to Italy. They also need a residency permit, to be obtained upon arrival in Italy by visiting the post office and police station. Those wishing to stay for more than 12 months may also have to sign a declaration of integration.

For more information, please visit the website www.schengenvisainfo.com/italy/visa/

Packing Tips

Packing is one of those things where either you are good at it, or you're someone who over- or under-packs for a trip. As you are packing for your travels, consider where you are going. Remember, the regions in Italy will not have the same temperature, so you'll want to be strategic in your packing to make it manageable. Your goal is to find a balance between being prepared and traveling light.

Before you start packing, make an essential packing list for one week and add some items based on the activities, season, and how long you'll be in Italy. These basics can include

- three tank tops
- three basic T-shirts
- three blouses or dress shirts
- one or two long sleeve shirts
- two pairs of jeans
- one lightweight jacket
- seven pairs of underwear or boxers
- seven pairs of socks
- two pairs of workout or yoga pants
- two sweaters (a cardigan and a hoodie or crew sweatshirt)
- sunglasses
- reusable water bottle
- comfortable walking shoes

Spring

In addition to the basics, consider packing one or two scarves and a travel-sized umbrella if you go to Italy in the spring.

Summer

For summer in Italy, the weather will be significantly warmer. However, remember that northern Italy will still be cooler in June and September:

- one sundress
- one skirt
- two pairs of shorts
- one to two swimsuits
- flip-flops and water shoes
- sunscreen
- hat
- waterproof phone pouch or a waterproof camera
- beach bag and towel

Autumn

If you are going to Italy between late September and November (even early December), you should consider packing the additional items:

- warm hat
- scarf
- extra long sleeve or sweater
- travel umbrella
- boots

Winter

If you travel to Italy between December and February, in addition to the items listed in the autumn section, you would want to carry a winter coat, gloves, or mitts.

This may seem like an overload of things to pack, but this is also where you can plan your outfits accordingly. However, checking the weather to see what you can expect over the next week or two of your trip will help you decide what you must have with you. Aiming to pack versatile is a good rule of thumb to follow. In addition, packing cubes are handy, but there are compressible bags you can also purchase on places like Amazon that can fit a significant number of clothes into them!

Toiletries and Other Things

It's always best to pack your toiletries, but if you forget anything, you can always visit a pharmacy (Farmacia) to pick up some of the little essentials:

- Advil or other over-the-counter pain relief medicine
- constipation medicine
- diarrhea medicine
- motion sickness medicine
- prescription medication
- shampoo and conditioner in travel-sized bottles
- face wash and moisturizer
- make-up (if you wear it)
- a bar of soap
- laundry detergent sheets (in case you need to wash something)
- universal travel adaptor suitable for European sockets
- a small foldable chair
- Ziploc bags to keep dirty clothes in if you won't be hand washing them

Carry-On Must-Haves

Aside from ensuring you have your passport on hand, here are some of the items you will want to have with you on the plane:

- sleep mask
- headphones
- socks
- light sweatshirt
- travel blanket and pillow
- tablet or your laptop
- camera
- phone charging cord
- hand cream

What NOT to Pack for Italy

Now that we have all of the essentials you should be packing, here is what not to bring:

- jewelry and other valuables that can easily be stolen
- high heels (there are far too many cobblestone streets in Italy to handle heels)
- things you may lose or forget, such as a big floppy hat
- hair dryers or other hair styling tools

Essential Travel Insurance Coverage

Travel insurance provides financial protection and peace of mind in case an unexpected event happens, ensuring that you will have a smoother and worry-free travel experience. Your travel insurance should include coverage for

- trip cancellation
- trip interruption
- trip delay
- medical expenses
- medical evacuation and baggage

When looking at travel insurance, ensure that you assess your needs for your trip and select a policy that will give you adequate coverage. You should also find the policy maximum, exclusions, claim processes, and the 24/7 number to contact the company if you require insurance assistance. I recognize that some people are planning their trips out in advance, so ensuring you have coverage that can allow you to cancel or delay if needed is essential.

Winter Sports Coverage

If you are going to Italy to ski or snowboard in the winter months, you must have winter sports liability insurance. This insurance covers injuries or if you cause damage to other people (though I hope you don't crash into someone). This type of insurance is not typically offered in United States travel plans, but you can purchase them at Italian ski resorts for about three euros per day per person.

In the event you encounter an emergency (though I certainly hope you don't), here are some contact numbers to keep in mind:

- **118:** medical emergencies
- **113:** general emergencies (similar to 911 in Canada and the States)
- **112:** national police (Carabinieri)
- **115:** fire department

Additionally, it's a good idea to note down the contact details of your country's embassy or the consulate in Italy.

Currency Exchange and Money-Saving Tips

Understanding currency exchange rates and implementing money-saving strategies can help you maximize your budget.

Italy's currency is the euro. If you want to get currency before you leave, you can visit a foreign currency exchange or your bank to pick up some cash to bring with you. Otherwise, some bankomats (the Italian version of an ATM) will accept your debit card to take money out. However, credit cards are also accepted in many hotels, shops, restaurants, and taxis throughout Italy.

If you intend to use your cards while in Italy, here are some additional things to keep in mind:

- Tell your bank about your travel dates and what cities you plan to use your debit or credit cards.
- Find out what your daily withdrawal limit is.
- Find out if your bank has partnerships with Italian branches to get free cash withdrawals.
- Find out about foreign transaction fees.

As for saving money while traveling around Italy, these hacks help you avoid breaking your budget for your trip! To recap, here are some things we discussed earlier in the chapter that can help to maximize your budget:

- Be flexible about your travel days.
- Decide if you will travel during peak or off-peak and shoulder seasons.
- Outside of those, here are some other money-saving hacks to consider on your trip:
- Use transportation such as trains and buses to get to and from the airport.
- If you rent a car, request one that runs on diesel.
- Take the slower train instead of the high-speed one.
- Get a transit card instead of paying for transit each time.
- Get a city card that can provide savings on admissions to attractions, public transportation, shops, and restaurants. The bonus is that city cards can often fast-track you to the front of the line at some museums!
- Take a free tour. Find out what days museums have free days.
- Consider staying outside of the city center.
- Rent an apartment instead of staying in a hotel. At least in an apartment, you can grocery shop and cook a little "at home" instead of eating out daily.
- If you eat out, look for restaurants offering prix fixe meals.
- If you are paying by card and are prompted to convert to U.S. currency (or wherever you are traveling from), don't. Banks and merchants will add a commission if you use their conversion service.

What to Avoid When Planning Your Italy Trip

There is plenty of information on how to plan your trip to Italy, and while a lot of it is primarily focused on the things you should do, we can't forget about the things you shouldn't avoid! (Or else this book wouldn't be called *What Not to Do in Italy*). So, without further ado, here are some mistakes and pitfalls you should avoid while planning your grand excursion! Most of these we have discussed, so consider it a reminder:

Don't skip the guided tours: Guided tours are fun! You get to learn from the experts about things you may not have learned alone!

Don't book last minute: If you plan your trip last minute, it can be costly. Try to start planning your trip at least six months ahead.

Don't omit to book skip-the-line tickets: Unless you want to stand in line for hours, book your tickets to tourist attractions in advance!

Please don't spend too much or too little time in Rome: Rome is a magnificent city in Italy, but it's not the only place to see. Depending on how long you are in Italy, spend no more than three days in Rome, checking out the attractions and leisurely wandering the city.

Don't try to fit everything in: If Rome wasn't built in a day, would you be able to see everything in Italy in a week or two? No. (Unless you are a time traveler, then sign me up!) Everyone travels at their own pace, but decide what is most important to you to see on your trip and be realistic by building in additional time for checking in and other things.

Don't Forget the Small Towns: The major cities in Italy are an obvious choice, but don't forget about the small towns! The little towns around the major cities have their own charm and history!

Don't overlook getting a local eSIM or SIM card: Roaming charges are hefty when you are out of your country. Purchase an eSIM or SIM card for Italy to avoid getting a big cell phone bill at the end of the month.

Don't skip out on public transportation: Renting a car is handy but costly! If you are sticking to a budget, use public transportation as often as possible.

Don't forget to become acquainted with local scams: Scams can happen everywhere. Some scams to be aware of are 1) overly friendly strangers keen to help you, 2) friendship bracelet scams, 3) taxi scams (watch out for cars that don't have a taxi sign)

Don't skip learning basic Italian phrases: Learning new languages is fun! In the glossary, you will find a complete list of essential words and phrases you can use.

Planning a trip to Italy may seem overwhelming, but this chapter provides valuable tips to make the process easier. When booking, consider the best time to go based on your desired activities and budget. Your choice of season can also impact flight and accommodation costs. Research the airports closest to your desired destinations and decide whether to stay in a hotel or elsewhere—book tickets in advance to save time and money. Check visa requirements for stays over 90 days. Pack versatile outfits suitable for the season. Understand currency rates and consider low-cost transportation options. Lastly, get a local SIM card, learn basic Italian phrases, and be aware of common scams. With these tips, you'll be prepared for an incredible trip to Italy!
Fai i bagagli! (Pack your bags!)

Chapter 2

Italy—Tips and Tricks

Did you know Italy has 58 world heritage sites (*Italy*, n.d.)? That's more than any other country in the world! Now that we have your trip planning underway let's discuss the tips and tricks about going to Italy, including navigating their transportation systems, fostering respectful behavior, following cultural etiquette, and other general tips while traveling in Italy.

Getting Around

Before embarking on your trip to Italy, it's helpful to familiarize yourself with the transportation system. The good news is that the infrastructure in Italy is top-notch, with trains, buses, ships, and ferries available to take you to any destination in the country. Having this knowledge will make your travels smoother and less stressful.

Public Transportation

If you plan to travel around Italy, their transportation system is convenient. To save time, consider taking the high-speed or late-night rail services. Additionally, some Italian cities have metro systems and several bus options. Alternatively, you can always opt for a taxi.

Route Planning Apps

To make commuting more manageable, you can use apps like Google Maps and Citymapper to plan your public transportation routes in Italy. These apps suggest the best transportation to reach your destination and tourist attractions. The Trenitalia app is recommended for train travel, as it is Italy's official train operator and offers route planning, service updates, and deals. You can use the Italo Treno app to save money on train tickets.

Traveling by Train

Italy's train system is a reliable way to explore the country managed by Rete Ferroviaria Italiana (RFI). High-speed trains can reach up to 186 miles per hour, while intercity trains offer a more affordable option with scenic countryside views. If you plan to use intercity trains, booking your tickets in advance through the app or at a train station counter or self-service machine can save you money. Regional train tickets can be purchased upon arrival at the station, but it's crucial to validate your ticket before boarding to avoid fines. Also, train stations provide timetables, route maps, and arrival/departure information, but an app is recommended to verify (plus, it's a portable way to check times). If you prefer a paper schedule, they are also available.

Traveling by Bus

Buses are an excellent choice for short trips within your city or region. While they may be slower than trains, most cities offer frequent bus services. If you plan to use the bus frequently, it's worth getting a bus pass (*abbonamento*) to save money. Otherwise, you can purchase bus tickets at convenience stores. Use apps like Google Maps for navigation to help you figure out which buses to take. Remember to pack your patience, given that the buses won't get you to your destination as quickly as the train!

Taxis, Ubers, or Other Car Services

If you cannot use public transportation to travel around Italy, you can find taxis in most major cities. To avoid being overcharged or carrying extra cash, you can use the itTaxi app to book your ride, see the fare, and make payments. Additionally, Uber is available in some parts of Italy, and you can check the app to see if it is an option for you.

If you want to rent a car instead but do not need one for the entirety of your trip, use a car-sharing alternative. Services such as CarpoolWorld and BlaBlaCar are excellent options for driving between cities.

Ferries

If you want a different scenic route, take a ferry to certain parts of Italy. Most ferries offer short distances as shuttle services; others provide an overnight ferry experience between islands further apart, such as traveling Sicily and Sardinia.

Something to keep in mind is that some ferries are seasonal. Ones between Naples and Positano run between May and September, while the ferries between Salerno and Amalfi run from April to October. Ferry Hopper is a great website to check out ferry schedules for your destinations.

In addition, the ferry services in Italy are not limited to the country; some can also take you to Croatia, Spain, Corsica, Greece, and Tunisia.

Planes

You need a plane to get you to Italy if you don't live in any surrounding European countries. But you may also want to take a plane to cover significant distances, such as traveling between Milan and Sicily. However, flying within the country is not always a convenient option. While budget airlines offer domestic plane services, the service is not so beneficial. If you are traveling a long distance, opt for a train ride (either the slow or high-speed one) because it might save you a headache!

Renting a Car

Renting a car in another country is sometimes scary when unfamiliar with driving in a foreign country. It can be a little more expensive to do this because of gas prices and tolls along the way. However, if you want to visit some Italian countryside towns and villages, getting to them without a car is a bit harder. Here are some cities and towns you may want to consider renting a car for if that is where you will be for a few days:

- Tuscany
- Puglia
- Sicily and Sardinia
- Umbria

If you decide to rent a car, you must be at least 21 and no older than 75. Here are other things you require for renting a car: a valid driver's license, passport, and a credit card.

In addition, you must purchase basic car rental insurance—it's mandatory in Italy, and you cannot drive a rental car in Italy without it. It's also wise to purchase an international driving permit. The car rental company may not ask for it, but if you were to be pulled over by the police, you would need one. The international driving permit can be purchased through AAA.

Driving Around

We won't get into the entire logistics of driving around in Italy; however, here are a couple of things to know:

Tolls: When you enter toll roads, you will get a ticket (like a parking ticket), which you must pay when you exit. Keep some cash on you as some tolls don't have working credit card machines.

Italian drivers are excellent but impatient: I guess there is a reason why some of the fastest cars were invented in Italy. If you aren't prepared to go the second the light turns green, be prepared to be honked at. The same reaction can happen when you are merging onto a highway. That said, please be safe and don't let the pressure of other drivers influence how you drive.

Cycling

Cycling around Italy is one of the greener options to consider, plus you can give yourself a self-guided tour along the way! Check out which cities offer easy bike rentals if this is an option you are interested in pursuing.

What NOT to Do When Getting Around Italy

Getting around a foreign country can feel overwhelming, especially for the first time going! In this section, we will look at all of the actions and behaviors you should avoid.

Don't Rely on the English Translation
English language options are available when you purchase train tickets from machines, but don't expect the same translation level if you need directions! Ensure you know the name of the destination you want to get to in Italian. For example, we pronounce "Rome" as we spell it. However, Italy pronounces it "Roma" (like the tomato).

Don't Expect Public Transportation to Be on Time
Every city that has public transportation has its flaws, and yes, you can expect that sometimes delays will happen. Regional trains that run between towns and cities tend to be slower and are often late. Plan extra buffer time when planning your itinerary to ensure you have enough time to catch the train and get to where you want to go.

Don't Forget to Validate Your Ticket
When you purchase a bus or train ticket, they can be used at any point as they do not have a set time or date. Therefore, remember to validate your ticket before boarding. Validation machines can be found near the platform or bus stop. If you forget to validate it, you could risk being fined.

Don't Use Your Hands to Hail a Cab
Unless you live in New York City or another city in the United States where you can use your hands to hail a cab, don't use this practice in Italy. You may look like a hilarious American to the on-looking Italians waving your hands about trying to get a cab's attention. Instead, wait by a cab stand (marked with an orange sign) or call for a taxi.

Don't Forget to Look Both Ways Before Crossing the Street
Well, this is one practice we learned from walking with our parents in the early days. However, we sometimes forget this practice nowadays, especially when looking at our phones. While you may be trying to figure out where you need to go, don't forget to look both ways before you cross the street to avoid getting hit by a car or Vespa. You can resume looking at your map app when you are safely on the other side.

Don't Expect Subways to Cover the Whole City
Some countries have excellent subway systems that cover the entire city, but don't expect that same coverage from Italy. If you intend to use as much public transportation as possible, try to stay in an Italian city with a subway system. However, your best option is to walk!

Don't Forget to Carry the Right Documents When Driving
If you rent a car, don't forget to keep the following in your glove compartment to show at checkpoints:

- passport
- international driving permit (IDP)
- local driver's license
- rental car documents (Keep these in the glove compartment!)

Don't Forget the Relevant Speed Limits
Speed limits are set for a reason. However, in Italy, the speeds do fluctuate based on driving conditions. For example, on a sunny day, the maximum speed limit on significant motorways is 80 miles per hour; on a rainy or snowy day, the speed limit is 70 miles per hour.

On regular inner city and town roads, the speeds vary based on whether it's a built-up area. Speed limits range between 55 and 88 miles per hour outside built-up areas, whereas inside built-up areas range between 31 and 43 miles per hour. Just be sure to pay attention to the posted signage to avoid getting caught by a speed camera.

Don't Talk on Your Phone While Driving
It may sound so basic, but it's very important. Distracted driving is one of the common reasons for accidents in any country. However, in Italy, talking on your phone while driving is forbidden (unless it's an emergency). However, there are emergency solution stops every 1.24 miles where you can call emergency services (ambulance, fire, or police), mechanical help (look for a button with a spanner icon), or medical help (a button with a red cross icon).

Don't Park in the Wrong Place

Most major cities have a blue road sign indicating a parking lot where you can park for a small fee. In some cities, you can park for free on Sundays (but ensure to double-check signage to indicate if this is the case).

You will also want to ensure your GPS doesn't accidentally take you into a *zona traffico limitato* (ZTL) (limited traffic area). These areas are around many historical sites, and driving in them can result in a significant fine. Cameras are set up at the entrance of ZTLs and will take a photo of your license plate, so ensure you do your research or ask your hotel if they have a ZTL map to help guide you on where you can park.

As for street parking, if the roadway is two-way, park on the right-hand side of the road. If it is one-way, you can park on either side as long as there is a three-meter (about 10 feet) gap down the middle.

Don't Forget to Take Note of Disability Parking Spots

If you have a disability, so long as you have a disability sticker to support this, you can access parking spaces designated for you. These spaces have a wheelchair and yellow lines. If this doesn't apply to you, don't park in that spot.

Don't Break the Rules

As you would do at home, follow the laws of Italy because if you get caught, you'll pay the price for it. (And that could be a serious damper on your trip!)

Safety

With Europe being (what seems like) a prime target for terror threats and Italy being infamous for its organized crime, it's natural to wonder if you'll be safe over there. Italy is safe, and the crime rates are significantly low, ranking 32 out of 163 for safety and peace compared to other countries around the globe (*Global Peace Index*, 2022).

Still, just as you would want to watch out for your safety at home, you should consider these safety measures while traveling in Italy.

Of the more apparent crimes you could encounter, pickpocketing, bag snatching, and other thievery could happen if you aren't mindful of your surroundings.

Many people love using belt bags because they are lightweight, but those buckles make it easy for a thief to take off with your things. So, a helpful hack is to zip-tie the buckle to prevent them from taking off with it. That said, keep your valuables close and in front of you to avoid pickpockets, and never leave your phone and wallet on the table while at a restaurant (inside and out). For men carrying wallets, minimize what you need in your wallet and keep your wallet in your front pocket.

It might feel weird, but it's much better than having someone sneakily slip it out of your back pocket while in line or taking transit.

Emergency and Assistance

In the first chapter, you were given a list of numbers to call if you require emergency assistance. Here are some other things to know:

Health care: If you need medical assistance, Italy will guarantee it to anyone who needs it. Remember that if you or someone has a medical emergency, call 118.
Criminal actions: Report theft, fraud, or violence to the Carabinieri (112) and police (113)
As a U.S. citizen, you should also ensure that your health coverage will cover you outside the States. Ensure you carry your insurance policy identity card to prove you are insured.

What NOT to Do When It Comes to Safety

This section will cover what you must be mindful of to keep yourself and your traveling partners or family safe.

Don't Leave Your Belongings Unattended

Whether abroad or at home, you should never leave your belongings unattended. Thieves are always looking for someone to leave their bags on a chair while someone runs to the restroom. Keep your stuff with you at all times.

Don't Display Expensive Items

Leave your expensive items at home. You don't want to be wearing things that could attract you as a potential wealthy person to steal from.

Don't Share Personal Information with Strangers

If you don't know the person, don't share personal information with them, such as where you are staying or your full name.

Don't Fall for Scams

If you are not aware of your surroundings, you could fall victim to any of these scams:

The Lira coin scam: Italy switched to the Euro currency in 2001. If you pay by cash and get change, ensure the coins say "EURO" on them.
Gypsies: Gypsies are almost always in groups (mainly women with a baby and other children), coming up and asking you for money. These kids are crafty and can pickpocket you easily because you can't keep track of their many hands. You may even find yourself suddenly holding a baby, which turns out to be a doll. The

kids may even shove a pizza box toward you to block your view of your pockets, purse, or other items.

Fake designer brands: Knock-offs are sold everywhere in Europe. They're often displaced on cardboard boxes or sheets if they need to escape quickly from the police. You could be okay with buying a fake designer brand, but many don't realize that on top of it being illegal to sell designer brands in Italy, it's also illegal to buy them. As a buyer, you could face a fine of 10,000 euros (about USD 11,000—significantly more than your trip should cost)!

Friendship bracelet scam: These scammers will hang out around popular tourist attractions holding a handful of friendship bracelets. They'll fasten one on you and demand money if you get too close. They can turn nasty quickly if you walk away without paying them.

Gold ring scam: The gold ring scam is similar to the friendship bracelet guys. Someone may walk up to you with a gold ring and ask if it's yours. When you say no, the person will walk away but return and say you should take it anyway. If you do and thank them, they'll demand money, and just like the friendship guys, it can turn nasty.

Taxi scam: Before getting into a taxi, ensure the meter works! If the driver says it's not, get out. On this note, never take unmarked taxis as they are illegal, and never follow the rules.

Don't Ignore Your Surroundings

This is a rule of thumb no matter where you are. Watch for people or areas that may be giving you bad vibes. If you're unsure of neighborhoods you should avoid, ask a tourist information office.

Respectful Behavior and Etiquette

The wonderful thing about traveling to a foreign country is the ability to experience a completely different way of living. But, as with every country, you should follow some rules and etiquette while in Italy to ensure you positively interact with the locals and navigate the cultural landscape with sensitivity.

Interacting With the Locals

While being in a foreign country where Italian likely isn't your first language, conversing with some locals may feel intimidating. However, you don't need to be fluent in Italian to communicate, but if you feel frustrated by not being able to understand them, don't get mad. Communication struggles are common in foreign countries, but you can get by with some basic phrases, which you can find in the glossary.

Remember that Italians are loud and vibrant individuals who take pride in caring for those around them. You will notice how warm and welcoming they are when you greet them and frequently smile. If you stay with an Italian family, remember to shake their hands and look in their eyes. While out and about, greet the locals with a smile. Above all, remember to be kind and mind your manners.

Historical and Sacred Sites

Some tourists lack common sense regarding visiting foreign countries, specifically historical and sacred sites.

When you go to visit churches, please understand that they have strict dress codes that everyone must follow. When visiting the churches, your knees and shoulders are expected to be covered, and you must wear proper shoes. If you're not dressed appropriately, you cannot enter the church. While in the church, remember to keep your voice low.

If you want to take a photo, be sensible about where you are taking it. For example, you don't want to take pictures in a graveyard commemorating war victims as this is a sign of disrespect. Additionally, don't snap photos of people in historical sites without their permission.

Dining and Culinary Etiquette

Food is central to Italy, but it is much more than just enjoying a delicious pasta dish or pizza pie. Italians are very proud of their dishes and treat their mealtimes with respect and special etiquette. Unlike traditional American life, where we seem to eat and run, Italians savor mealtime with their families, making their way through several courses.

While eating at restaurants, do not dig into your food until the waiter or host says, "*Buòn appetito!*" When you pay for a meal, you're not expected to leave a tip, but if you feel inclined because you had great food and service, 10% is more than enough!

Behavior and Etiquette: What NOT to Do

In this section, let's explore what you should avoid in order to demonstrate the utmost respect in Italy. In terms of general things, remember not to

- make generalized comments surrounding Italian crime, the Mafia, or their involvement in the Second World War.
- make jokes about the Pope or the Catholic Church.
- draw on Italian cultural stereotypes when chatting with Italians.
- forget to dress appropriately if visiting churches or other sacred si
- talk with your mouth full.
- burp or slurp loudly.
- eat or drink at any famous site in all cities.
- fly drones in urban areas—you need a license or a permit.

Don't Say "Ciao" When You First Meet Someone
While "Ciao" means hello or goodbye, it's a greeting used among people who know one another well. Instead, use phrases such as *buongiorno* and *buona sera*.

Don't Overconsume Alcohol
Yes, Italians enjoy their wines throughout the day, but don't overconsume them. Drinks with antipasti, bread, and meals are meant to be enjoyed slowly. Appearing drunk and sloppy in public will not make many locals happy.

Don't Sprinkle Parmigiana Everywhere
Grated cheese is delicious on your risotto or pasta, but Italians never use parmigiana on dishes containing fish, seafood, salads, and pizza. A general rule of thumb: If your waiter does not offer grated cheese, your dish doesn't require it.

Don't Drink Alcohol Out of Glass Containers in Public
In Rome, you cannot drink alcohol from glass containers on public streets, in public transit, or in non-enclosed green spaces after 10 p.m. After midnight, you are not permitted to drink in these spaces, period.

Italy's transportation system can appear daunting, but this chapter has equipped you with the knowledge to move seamlessly between destinations. Awareness of cultural etiquette is essential to ensure sensitivity toward locals and enhance your travel experience. With preparation and cultural sensitivity in mind, it's time to begin exploring this beautiful country, starting with one of my favorites, Milan!

Chapter 3

Milan—Dos and Don'ts

Milan, or Milano, as the locals call it, is the first stop in our book! Home to some of the most impressive sights and an annual Christmas market called "Oh Bej! Oh Bej!" hosted at the Castello Sforzesco, Milan is a vibrant city in Lombardy, Italy, known for its rich history, fashion, and cultural history.

But it's much more than its fun Christmas market! Milan has a rich and complex history that spans several centuries. Various groups once ruled it, including the Celtics, Romans, Goths, Lombards, Spaniards, and Austrians. Milan became a part of the Roman Empire in 222 B.C.E. and played a central role until the Empire's decline. After the fall of the Empire, the Visconti family ruled Milan from 1277 to 1447, contributing to the city's wealth and cultural heritage.

Then, in 1450, the Sforza family gained control, sparking Milan's development. Francesco Sforza turned Milan into a significant metropolis by constructing the Duomo di Milano and Castello Sforzesco. Ludovico Sforza furthered Milan's cultural and economic progress by attracting architects like Leonardo da Vinci, making Milan a prominent city in Italian culture.

What to DO in Milan

Milan is one of the top fashion and design capitals of the world. Although it is a busy city that takes many initiatives, it holds its history and traditions to its core. Here are some things you should check out while you are in Milan.

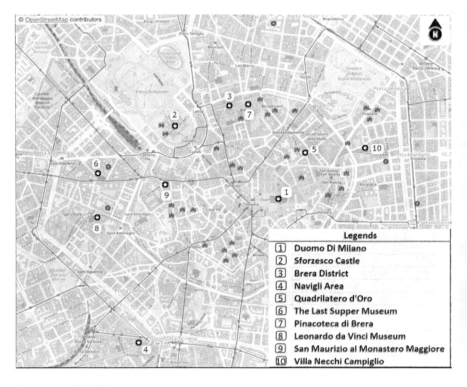

Legends

1	Duomo Di Milano
2	Sforzesco Castle
3	Brera District
4	Navigli Area
5	Quadrilatero d'Oro
6	The Last Supper Museum
7	Pinacoteca di Brera
8	Leonardo da Vinci Museum
9	San Maurizio al Monastero Maggiore
10	Villa Necchi Campiglio

Duomo di Milano

Hours of operation: 9 a.m. to 7 p.m. daily

Please note that each area may have different hours of operation and when the final entry time is. It is best to check out the official website when pre-booking your tickets. You will also notice there are some reduced rates. These rates apply to children between 6 and 18 years old as well as religious groups. Children aged 0 to 5 and people with disabilities with personal carers are free. The information is from the Duomo di Milano website (*Tickets*, n.d.)

Duomo di Milano is one of the biggest Gothic cathedrals in Italy, taking over six centuries to complete.

Area	Price
Terrace evening opening with lift access	€15 (reduced €7,50)
Duomo Terraces Museum with lift access	€22 (reduced €11)
Duomo Terraces Museum (stair access)	€16 (reduced €8)
Duomo and Ambrosiana	€30 (reduced €20)
Fast track passes with access to terraces by lift	€28 (reduced €14)
Fast track lift terraces access only	€24 (reduced €12)
Duomo and museum access only	€8 (reduced €4)
Terraces only with lift access	€15 (reduced €7,50)
Terraces only (stair access)	€13 (reduced €6,50)
Culture pass	€10 (reduced €5)

As you approach this magnificent sacred site, take in its pinkish-white marble and the golden statue of the Madonnina on the highest spire. Inside the cathedral, you will see gorgeous stained-glass windows to show biblical scenes and a solar sundial constructed in 1789 by the Brera Astronomical Observatory.

If you want to take the elevator up to the Terraces, you'll be granted the opportunity to see the spires and Madonnina up close while getting a stunning panoramic view of Milan.

Castello Sforzesco

Hours of operation: 9 a.m. to 5:30 p.m. daily

Admission to the castle is free. However, if you want to visit the museums, the admission fee is €5 (€3 for visitors between 18 and 25 years old and 65 and up). There is free admission to the museums every first and third Tuesday from 2 p.m. until closing and every first Sunday of the month.

The Castello Sforzesco is one of Milan's largest European castles and a tourist attraction. At the time of its construction between 1300 and 1400, the palace was mainly a defensive function. Today, it's the home to civic museums, hosting various works by Bellini, Antonello da Messina, and Mantegna. In addition, it's an Egyptian museum, the Museum of Ancient Art, the home of Michelangelo's unfinished sculpture, and the Pinacoteca and the Sala delle Asse by Leonardo Davinci.

Outside of the castle walls, enjoy walking through the three gorgeous courtyards that surround the castle: the Piazza d'Armi, Rocchetta, and the Ducal Court.

If you visit Milan during Christmas, check out the "Oh Bej! Oh Bej!" festival! This event is one of the oldest in Italy, tracing back to 1288 when celebrations took place to honor the Patron Saint. Today, it's an event with various vendors selling antiques, bric-a-brac, clothing, toys, Christmas decor, sweets, and other winter treats.

Brera District

In the Brera District, prepare to be charmed by its history. This area is referred to as the artists' district as it became the home of the Academy of Fine Arts,

constructed in 1776 at the request of Empress Maria Theresa of Austria. Since the 19th century, Brera has become an artist's dream destination, shaping it into what it is today. Visiting the Academy of Fine Arts is a must. However, seeing the Palazzo Brera, the National Gallery of Ancient and Modern Art, the Braidense National Library, the Instituto Nazionale di Astrofisica (INAF) Astronomical Observatory, and the Botanical Garden should also be up there in your wanderings of this area.

Brera is home to art, and if you enjoy unique fashion trends, check out the various fashion boutiques for distinctive garments and bohemian-style design studios.

Navigli Area

The Navigli area begins at the Darsena in Porta Ticinese, where two waterways

branch off. If you're into nightlife experiences, this spot is filled with trendy nightclubs, bars, and small shops among the mix of art nouveau, modern buildings, and famous railing houses.

While here, stroll the bridges over the canals and wander through the various alleys to look at the large, old wooden doors! This area has so many contrasts that it is one area you don't want to miss, especially at night!

Quadrilatero Della Moda (Fashion District)

Fashion lovers unite! Along the streets of Via Monte Napoleone, Via Della Spiga,

Via Manzoni, and Corso Venezia, you will find shops dedicated to luxury shopping experiences. In this district, walk along the streets to window shop and visit showrooms devoted to showing unique tastes and designs.

This district also contains various museums showcasing fashion, costume, and images, such as the Casa Museo Valsecchi, Casa del Manzoni, Casa Museo Poldi Pezzoli, and Gallerie d'Italia and Palazzo Morando.

Museum of the Last Supper

Hours of operation: Sunday from 2 p.m. to 7 p.m. and Tuesday to Saturday from 8:15 a.m. to 7 p.m. This museum is closed on Mondays.

Admission fees: €15 (reduced €2). All tickets must be pre-booked.

When you visit the Museum of the Last Supper, you will be immersed in an extraordinary experience as you view much of Leonard da Vinci's art. You can view the famous The Last Supper painting at this museum, and it is the one painting that should not be missed on your travels. It represents Italy's rich history, art, and culture, in addition to da Vinci's elevated artistic career during the Renaissance.

Pinacoteca di Brera

Hours of operation: Tuesday to Sunday from 8:30 a.m. to 7:15 p.m. (last entrance time is at 6:15 p.m.). This museum is closed on Mondays.

Admission fees: €15 (reduced €2 for citizens of the European community aged between 18 and 25 years)

The Pinacoteca di Brera is one of Italy's biggest art galleries, founded in 1809 by Napoleon I. This gallery houses various Tuscan, Lombard, and Venetian paintings from the Renaissance and Baroque periods, including works by Tiepolo, Tintoretto, Piero della Francesca, and Caravaggio. Feel free to roam the museum on your own to check out the masterpieces, but you can book guided tours too!

Museum of Science and Technology

The hours of operation vary per season. Depending on when you are going, you should check the museum's website to verify their operation hours and book your tickets in advance.

Admission fees: €10 (reduced €7,50 for kids and young adults aged 3 to 26 years old and adults 65 and up with proof of birth). Any children under 3 are free. If you wish to follow a guided tour, it's €90 for 55 minutes or €150 for an hour and 50 minutes plus admission.

Visiting the Leonardo da Vinci National Museum of Science and Technology is a must if you are looking for an entertaining and comprehensive way to get to know da Vinci as a scientist and engineer. You will get to walk through and learn about all of his inventions and his love of exploration. In addition, there are many interactive workshops you and your kids can enjoy as you learn to use gears to create your mechanical inventions. This was one of my favorite museums because it allowed everyone to understand how innovative da Vinci was!

San Maurizio al Monastero Maggiore

Hours of operation: Monday to Sunday from 9 a.m. to 12 p.m. and 2 p.m. to 5 p.m.

Admission is free.

The San Maurizio al Monastero Maggiore church was created for the Benedictine convent, Milan's most prominent congregation. This church has a stunning interior, with preserved walls from the sixteenth century. This church also houses an interesting secret: a temple split into two so that the citizens of Milan could sit near the entrance while the nuns sat on the other side, allowing many to come together to worship and pray.

Villa Necchi Campiglio

Hours of operation: Wednesday to Sunday from 10 a.m. to 6 p.m.

Admission fees: €15 (reduced €9 for visitors between 6 and 18 and students up to

25 years old). Children up to 5 years old can enter for free. If you are coming as a family with two adults and two or more children between 6 and 18, the fee is €39.

Additionally, the Villa Necchi Campiglio offers one-hour guided tours for €21 (reduced €15).

The Villa Necchi Campiglio was designed and built in the late 20th century by Milanese architect Piero Portaluppi. This exceptional work of architecture features original furniture, well-preserved collections, and several constructive and decorative elements, from the tennis court to the greenhouse and everything in between! It's an amazing way to step back into an entirely different world than we know today.

Things to Experience and Enjoy in Milan

While museums are excellent ways to immerse yourself in the rich history of Milan, you may want to check out some of the other experiences in the city, adding a uniqueness to your trip!

Teatro alla Scala (La Scala Opera House)

Inaugurated in 1778, the Teatro alla Scala was built upon the ashes of the former Teatro Ducale theater that had burned down years earlier by Austrian Empress Maria Tempress.

Draped in stunning velvet, this opera house became the hub for Italian melodrama in 1812 but became more famous after Gioachino Rossini debuted his greatest operas on the stage. Eventually, the theater expanded its scope to include ballet performances. The theater still offers opera and ballet performances today, which is worth checking out! However, you can also take a guided tour. If the tour interests you, you must visit La Scala's website to find out when tours are offered.

Aperitivo in Navigli or Brera

One of the traditions in Italian cuisine is to enjoy an *aperitivo*, a drink before the meal. This drink is traditionally made with Prosecco, Aperol, and sparkling water. Here are some spots to try out this drink in the Navigli and Brera districts:

Navigli

La Prosciutteria: If you love cheese and cold cuts, you can enjoy an aperitivo with a delicious spread of meat, cheese, and much more! This spot is very homelike, and many locals enjoy eating at La Prosciutteria!

Mag Cafe: Enjoy an aperitivo or other unique cocktails at this bar in this charming atmosphere. If you're not a fan of cocktails, they have an excellent wine selection in addition to Italian and international dishes.

Tenoha and Ramen: Aperitivo and ramen? Unlike any other bar, this restaurant is a furniture and hardware store offering an aperitivo experience! While enjoying your drink, pick up a bento box filled with Japanese street food and enjoy the outdoor area described as an oasis.

Brera

Pandenus Mercato: Step into this trendy location to enjoy an aperitivo, cocktail, or wine with some delicious eats!

La Tartina: This restaurant has a kitchen open all day and serves fresh slices of bread, meats, vegetables, sauces, cheeses, and fish to enjoy with your aperitivo! This restaurant's recipes are typically Venetian, but they change their menu often to follow the rhythms of the area.

La Casa Iberica: At La Casa Iberica, immerse yourself in a Spanish-influenced experience while enjoying your aperitivo! The stunning interior of this restaurant includes dark wood tables and intense green plants. Here, you can enjoy an array of tapas, including fish, meat, vegetables, cocktails, Spanish wines, and sangria!

Fashion Events During Milan Fashion Week

As Italians are well-known for their impeccable styles, many people jet set to Milan to see the stunning styles designers have created for fashion events! However, there's more than just the fashion shows! In the Quadrilatero della Moda area, many locations that aren't usually open to the public allow visitors to view art foundations and other historical palaces.

Gelato Tasting

Unless you have lactose issues, you must try gelato! While many may think it's ice cream, gelato is very different, made with more milk than cream. What's more, ice cream typically contains egg yolks, but gelato does not, which helps to give it its rich and dense texture. Here are some of the top places to taste gelato:

Artico Gelateria: This gelato place has an outstanding balance between classic and innovative flavors for gelato! If you're a chocoholic—this is the place for you as they have over ten different chocolate flavors and themes for your chocolate fix!

Ciacco: Ciacco is just steps from Duomo di Milano. Their gelato is created with high-quality ingredients locally sourced from the Lombard and Emilian regions. These gelato options have many interesting flavors you may not have considered mixing together!

Cerdini and Quenardel—Gelato e Champagne: The gelateria is near Duomo di Milano! Made with the highest-quality ingredients, you will find classic gelato flavors. However, the star of their gelato shop is their champagne-infused gelato! It's something you won't find anywhere else!

Football at the San Siro Stadium

Football to Europe and the United Kingdom is soccer to us! The San Siro Stadium

is iconic, hosting over 80,000 football fans watching Milan's soccer team play a match every Sunday. The energy is impressive during the games. However, you can also take tours organized by the stadium to see the behind-the-scenes!

Indro Montanelli Gardens (Public Park)

Hours of operations: 6:30 a.m. to 11:30 p.m. daily

Inaugurated in 1786, the Indro Montanelli Gardens is one of the oldest public parks in Milan. At the time of its inauguration, the gardens were created to reclaim the depressed Porta Venezia area; however, it was named Indro Montanelli in 2002 after the essayist and journalist of the same name who spent much of his free time walking among the avenues of the garden. Designed as a "French garden," the

Indro Montanelli Gardens has many flowerbeds, tree-lined avenues, and areas to exercise or play sports.

Parco Sempione

Hours of operation: 6:30 a.m. to 9 p.m.

Parco Sempione is a green oasis in the center of Milan, allowing locals and tourists to immerse themselves in nature in the city. Access this park through the Arco Della Pace and head toward Castello Sforzesco. However, if you're looking for a quiet, romantic moment with your love, stroll over the Little Mermaid bridge.

Rooftop Terraces with Panoramic Views

Earlier in this chapter, we touched briefly on the terraces at the Duomo di Milano. However, this is one experience that you should consider adding to your itinerary while at the cathedral! After climbing the 251 steps to the top (or taking the elevator), you can view Milan and its stunning beauty from an unmatched panoramic view (especially if you go at dusk)!

Dining at a Traditional Trattoria Restaurant

Trattoria restaurants are excellent places to dine on simple, authentic Italian dishes accompanied by delicious homemade wine. Trattoria restaurants are typically family-owned and run, offering a different dining experience that's intimate and cozy! Some restaurants to consider dining at are Antica Trattoria della Pesa, Osteria Conchetta, Trattoria del Nuovo Macello, Trattoria Masuelli San Marco, and Trattoria Madonnina.

I would recommend these dishes to try in Milan.

Risotto alla Milanese: This Milanese dish is a risotto infused with creamy

saffron. This is usually served with bone marrow and parmesan cheese to create an excellent, flavorful combination.

Ossobuco alla Milanese: It's a classical Milanese specialty dish. Ossobuco is a  braised veal shank cooked with vegetables, white wine, and broth. It's served with gremolata, a mixture of lemon zest, garlic, and parsley. This can also be enjoyed with saffron risotto.

Panettone: Panettone is a festive sweet bread that originated in Milan. It's  enjoyed during the Christmas season but can be found year-round. This fluffy bread is studded with raisins, candied fruits, and chocolate, creating a tasty dessert.

Staying in Milan

While visiting Milan, where you stay depends entirely on the type of experience you want. When choosing a place to stay, consider what sightseeing points you want to visit or the activities you want to engage in. Thankfully, Milan has an excellent public transportation system in case some of these points of interest need to be added to where you are staying. This section is just a quick overview of the best neighborhoods.

Navigli

Navigli is a bustling area at night for people who want to experience the nightlife. However, this area is quiet during the day, with a casual vibe where you can experience the restaurants lining the canals and some cute cafes, artsy boutiques, and bookshops. Here are some places you should check out for accommodations:

Combo Milano: The Combo Milano hotel is great for budgets and offers a more modern-day look in the rooms with plenty of light throughout. If you are looking for a hostel experience, the Combo Milano offers dormitories and private rooms. It's also near the Porta Genova Train Station to take you to Milan.

Art Hotel Navigli: The Art Hotel Navigli has several modern art sculptures and paintings throughout the building. It's steps away from the Porta Genova Metro Station, which will take you into Milan's city center. Once you return from your adventures, you can relax in their garden or terrace!

Brera

Brera is the central part of Milan, making it perfect as it's closer to everything. It is a more historic area of Milan, but it has a bit of a modern twist, especially at night when the bars are open! This area also has several family-friendly hotels if you are traveling with kids. Here are some of the places you should check out if you want to stay in Brera:

Antica Locanda Dei Mercanti: The Antica Locanda Dei Mercanti is a family-friendly hotel boasting beautiful rooms. The hotel is close to Milan's Castello Sforzesco. It's also near an exclusive shopping area and other tourist sights.

Locanda Pandenus: The Locanda Pandenus hotel offers spacious modern rooms and is excellent for two travelers. It's close to several points of interest, including the Duomo di Milano and the Museum of Science and Technology with Leonardo da Vinci.

Arco della Pace

Arco della Pace is another central area close to various tourist attractions in Milan. However, this area has a lovely green space near Parco Sempione. This area is excellent for families looking for a quiet area that's still pretty close to sightseeing points and activities. Here are a couple of places to look into for accommodations in Arco della Pace:

Sweet Inn: The Sweet Inn offers apartment-sized rooms with a kitchenette. It's near several attractions, including the Sforzesco Castle, The Last Supper, and other art galleries.

Pink Ladies of the World: A studio apartment in the Chinatown District of Milan, the Pink Ladies of the World is excellent for two travelers. It has a washing machine on-site, a balcony, a fridge, a freezer, and funky pops of color throughout.

San Lorenzo

The San Lorenzo neighborhood is located south of the Duomo di Milano Cathedral and offers a quiet area near the city center. If you stay here, you can easily access the cathedral and other tourist attractions. However, as it is relatively central, expect to pay a bit of a higher price for your accommodation. You can also expect to find more apartment-type accommodations versus a hotel like this one:

AgriCesar: The AgriCesar offers an apartment for your comfort, complete with two bedrooms, a bathroom, a full kitchen, and terrace and garden views. This place is excellent to stay in if you are traveling with family.

Porta Nuova

Porta Nuova is in the northern part of Milan. It's a slightly hidden neighborhood that was once an industrial area. There are several dining spots, trendy bars, and chic boutiques to check out while staying here. Here are a couple of places you should look into for accommodations:

Best Western Crystal Palace Hotel: Set in a 19th-century building, this hotel is on a lively street near several restaurants and bars. It's also near several exciting attractions, including the Egyptian Museum, Palazzo Madama, and Piazza Castello.
Attic Hostel: Although this accommodation is a hostel, it is kid-friendly if you plan to travel to Italy with your family! At this hostel, you'll stay in the attic of a neoclassical building, but there are several restaurants and bars in the area. In addition, you will be close to public transportation and attractions.

What NOT to Do in Milan

Common mistakes travelers can make while in Milan include simple miscalculations to inattention. Mistakes happen, but you should know what not to do while you stay in Milan to ensure your experience and time in the city are stress-free and enjoyable.

Don't Forget to Purchase a MilanoCard City Pass
The MilanoCard city pass is the easiest way to access Milan's public transportation. You can purchase the city pass for up to three days, giving you special discounts on city tours and some of Milan's top attractions!

Don't Touch Fresh Goods at the Market
If you have opted to stay at an apartment, you'll likely cook some meals "at home" and purchase fresh market goods. While shopping there, you may see signs indicating not to touch their fruits and vegetables. Remember, Italians are prideful, and picking through their produce may make it seem like you don't trust the quality. Allow the shopkeeper to pick them out based on your preferred ripeness and variety.

Don't Drive on Weekends
If you're in Milan over a weekend, using a rental car is discouraged since it's busier! Opt to use public transportation to get around the city instead.

Don't Forget the Areas to Avoid
While Milan is safe to visit, there are some neighborhoods you should avoid due to violence, drug trafficking, and general insecurity. They are Corvetto, Lambrate, Quarto Oggiaro, Giambellino-Lorenteggio, San Siro (unless you are going for a game or a tour of the stadium), and Via Gola, via Pichi e via Borsi.

Don't touch the artwork or exhibits.
Milan is home to renowned art galleries and museums. When visiting these cultural institutions, refrain from touching the artwork or exhibits. Follow any instructions provided to protect these treasures.

Don't Overlook Petty Crime and Scams
While I hope you have a safe trip in Milan, never let your guard down to things that seem off or sketchy. Be aware of any pretty crimes and scams that could affect your trip, such as pickpocketing, fake petitions, and transportation scams.

Milan is a beautiful city to begin your journey, with its lively atmosphere and historic locations. However, it's important to remember what you should and shouldn't do while you're there. You don't want to miss out on some of the great sites Milan has to offer, such as the Duomo di Milano and its terraces, Castello Sforzesco, and the Quadrilatero d'Oro, all of which are rich in history and full of amazing sights. Milan also offers the opportunity to delve into the world of Leonardo da Vinci at the museum, home to his famous painting, The Last Supper.

While traveling, experience some authentic Italian activities, like visiting the Teatro alla Scala Opera House, enjoying an aperitivo, and dining at a traditional trattoria restaurant. These experiences will give you a taste of the local way of life. When planning your trip, choose an area that suits your needs and budget. Milan has an excellent transportation system, and utilizing the city pass card will make your travels seamless.

Now that we have explored Milan, it's time to move on to the Cinque Terre, a picturesque area known for its charming villages and mouth-watering seafood dishes.

Chapter 4

Cinque Terre — Dos and Don'ts

C inque Terre or Cinqueterre (cheen-kweh teh-rreh) is a picturesque coastal area along the northwest side of Italy known as Liguria. Between December 8 and January 29, the front hill in the village of Manarola becomes the backdrop for a Nativity Scene with 17,000 lightbulbs and 300 life-sized figures setting the scene. This famous tradition began in 1961 when Mario Andreoli, a retired railway worker, began creating 4,000 square-meter art pieces. The figurines are made from recycled materials, plastic boxes, shutters, iron threads, and other materials. Thousands of people love to visit Manarola in Cinque Terre every holiday season to take in the stunning scene! There is nothing like it anywhere else!

What to DO in Cinque Terre

Outside of the stunning illuminated nativity scene in the Manarola village, Cinque Terre is stunning, with colorful buildings all along the hills squished together. Cinque Terre is 11 miles long on the eastern Ligurian Riviera. It has five linked villages, several hiking trails, and stunning ocean views. Its natural beauty leaves all visitors in awe, but people love this coastline for its beaches, bays, and sandy and pebble beaches. This destination is especially great for travelers who love to hike and be outdoors. Let's look at some things you should do while in Cinque Terre.

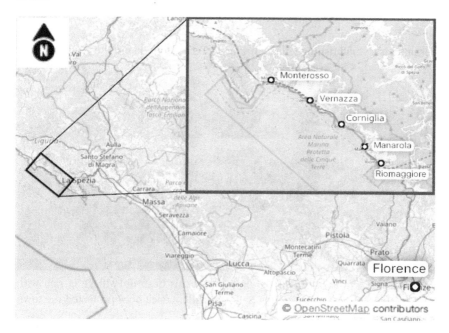

Monterosso al Mare

Monterosso al Mare is the biggest of the five villages in Cinque Terre. This village

is the easiest to walk around due to its flat terrain. However, it's not the attractions or landmarks that attract tourists, but rather the breathtaking sights and Fegina Beach along the coast. In addition to the beaches, some must-see spots in Monterosso include

- Church of San Giovanni Battista
- Statue of Neptune
- Castle Torre Aurora
- Convent of the Capuchin Friars
- San Francesco Church

- Sanctuary of Our Lady Soviore
- Villa Montale

Vernazza

Vernazza is a small fishing village in Cinque Terre. Founded in the year 1000 and

once ruled by the Republic of Genoa in 1276, this beautiful village is rich with history, complete with the famous Belforte castle, which once protected the town from pirates.

You can hike from Monterosso al Mare to Vernazza. However, you'll require a Cinque Terre Card. This card allows you to hike or to hike and use the train. Here are the current costs:

Card type	Hiking		Hiking and train		
	One day	Two days	One day	Two days	Three days
Adults (12 to 69 years old)	€7,50	€14,50	€18,20	€ 33	€ 47
Children (4 to 11 years old)	€4,50	€7,20	€11,40	Not available	Not available
Seniors 70 years old and up	€ 6	€ 10	€14,80	Not available	Not available

All cards are valid until midnight. Children between 0 and 3 years of age are free. In addition to hiking and taking in the stunning scenes from up above, be sure to check out some of these other spots: Church of Santa Margherita di Antiochia, Doria Castle, Santuario Nostra Signora di Reggio, Convento dei Padri Riformati di San Francesco, and Piazzetta del Porto

Corniglia

Corniglia is in the center of Cinque Terre, set at the top of a sheer cliff. It's the only

village that does not have direct access to the ocean! You can reach it by foot or by bus that leaves every 10 minutes after the train arrives. Remember, you'll need a ticket for the train!

This is the village that is well known for its hiking trails, so it's perfect if this is an interest for you! However, you should also check out the following places in the village: Church of San Pietro, Lardarina Staircase, and Santa Maria Terrace.

Manarola

Manarola looks something like a painting in real-time. Located in the center of

Cinque Terre and 70 meters above sea level, Manarola has yellow and orange houses standing out from the dark cliffs behind them. Interestingly, when Manarola was founded in the year 1000, its position was explicitly chosen as it was

a good lookout point for those pesky pirates! Here are some of the sites you should check out: the Church of San Lorenzo, La Via dell'Amore, and the ruins of the fortress of Manaorola.

And, of course, if you come here between December 8 and January 29, you can see the nativity scene!

Riomaggiore

Riomaggiore is the southern village in Cinque Terre and about a two-minute train

ride from Manarola. If you walk down the main street, you'll reach the small harbor surrounded by pretty pastel homes and bright-colored fishing boats. You can also check out a pebble beach near the docking point of the harbor.

For hiking, a 2.1-mile circular trail begins and ends in Riomaggiore. It climbs up to the church called the Santuario di Nostra Signora di Montenero from the 11th century. It's not open to visitors, but you can check out other views from the vineyards! Some other places you should see while in Riomaggiore include Riomaggiore Castle, Church of San Giovanni Battista, and Guardiola Tower of Riomaggiore.

Things to Experience and Enjoy in Cinque Terre

Though Cinque Terre is a smaller region in Italy, you can still experience many great things. (Even if taking hikes is not your thing!)

Boat Rides Along the Coast

You honestly cannot fully picture Cinque Terre while standing on foot. Sure, you can take in the colors of each small village, but it's from the sea where you can marvel at its beauty!

Taking a ferry that runs between the villages is one way to take in the colors and vibrancy of Cinque Terre. The ferries run between the end of March and the start of November at scheduled times. The only spot where the ferry doesn't stop is in Corniglia since this village does not have water access. Here are the current costs for ferry boat tickets (CinqueTerre.eu.com, 2023):

Boat ticket types	Adults	Children (6 to 11 years old)
One-day roundtrip	€ 39	€ 15
Afternoon roundtrip (from 2 p.m.)	€ 28	€ 15
One-way ticket with stops	€ 30	€ 15

Please note that children under six years old are free.

Another way to enjoy Cinque Terre's stunning sites from the water is by a private boat tour, which allows you to view Cinque Terre without the busyness of other tourists. Some things to keep in mind:

- The water is rough, so you may not enjoy it if you suffer from seasickness.
- A day trip isn't recommended for boat travel. While the villages are small, moving between each area takes some time.
- Most boat tours depart from La Spezia.

Lastly, an exclusive region tour on the historic boat, Luedo, is another excellent way to see Cinque Terre. On this tour, the captain will explain how he restored the boat and its initial purpose of transporting wine barrels along the Liguria and Tuscany coasts. This tour is excellent for groups of 6 people.

Walk Along the Blue Path

The Blue Path is a 7.45-mile trail suitable for almost everyone (there are a few difficult spots). The trail's starting point begins in Riomaggiore and moves through to Manarola. Remember to stroll through the villages for a quick bite between each stop or enjoy an aperitivo by the sea!

At the time of writing this book, the Blue Path Trail is closed but is expected to reopen to the public in 2024 (*The Blue Path*, n.d.). Also, note that you must pay an entry fee to access the trail. However, it's best to obtain that information when it reopens.

Seafood and Other Eats

The Cinque Terre is an excellent spot for people who love seafood! Ligurian cuisine (also known as *la cucina profumata*) is stunning, with colorful vegetables, herbs, garlic, and lemon. At the small, local restaurants, feast on some freshly caught fish and shellfish. I will recommend the following delicacies to try in Cinque Terre.

Frittura di Pesce (Mixed Seafood Fry): Frittura di Pesce is a popular seafood

dish in Italy, and it's a must-try in Cinque Terre. It typically includes a variety of local seafood such as anchovies, calamari, shrimp, and small fish, which are lightly battered and deep-fried to perfection. The result is a crispy and flavorful assortment of seafood that highlights the freshness of the Mediterranean ingredients.

Trofie al Pesto di Acciughe (Trofie Pasta with Anchovy Pesto): Trofie is a type

of hand-rolled pasta that is often served with a variety of sauces in Ligurian cuisine. One of the local specialties in Cinque Terre is Trofie al Pesto di Acciughe, which features trofie pasta tossed in a pesto made from anchovies, garlic, olive oil, and pine nuts. The anchovy pesto adds a unique and savory flavor to the dish, making it a delightful seafood-based pasta option.

Risotto alla Vernazza (Vernazza-style Risotto): Vernazza is one of the five

towns of Cinque Terre and is renowned for its seafood. Risotto alla Vernazza is a specialty of the region, featuring a creamy risotto cooked with a rich seafood broth and mixed with a variety of local seafood such as shrimp, clams, mussels, and squid. The dish showcases the flavors of the sea and the traditional culinary techniques of Cinque Terre.

In addition to some of these other yummy eats:

Pesto: Did you know Liguria is the birthplace of pesto? Pesto is delicious on pasta and bread as it is, but in Cinque Terre, it's even more special as they have their own variety of basil that is more citrusy and less minty!

Focaccia: This type of bread is my favorite—pair it with some olive oil and balsamic vinegar, and I'm in carb heaven! Okay, I'm off-topic here, but focaccia is a favorite among the locals. What I didn't know is that some love to dip it in their cappuccino! I tried it myself, and while the concept is weird, it's delicious!

Aperitivo at Nessun Dorma in Manarola

After you complete a hike or enjoy a dip in the ocean, head up to the Nessun Dorma, a wine bar that overlooks Manarola, to enjoy an aperitivo, a light snack, lunch, or dinner. Nessun Dorma offers an array of bruschetta, a mixed cheese platter, salami, buffalo mozzarella, burrata cheese, pesto, and Ligurian crostinis. This bar is open daily between 3:30 p.m. and 9 p.m. (except on Tuesdays) between March and November. If you plan to stop by, download their app to see how many people are waiting ahead of you.

Spend the Day at the Beach in Monterosso

Monterosso is the largest village of the five, so you shouldn't be surprised to find a long, stunning beach with white sand in this area! Several sunbeds are available with umbrellas to rent for your beach lounging pleasure; when you get a little toasty from the Mediterranean sun, take a dip in the crystal-clear ocean! You can also rent standup paddle boards here if you want to add some exercise to your beach day.

Enjoy Cinque Terre Wine

Wine in Italy is a historical tradition they enjoy with every meal! However, enjoying wine in Cinque Terre has a different meaning behind its delicious taste.

Cinque Terre wines are more earthy tasting as their vineyards are much more organic. As Cinque Terre is rocky and steep, it is more challenging to manage to create wines, so the harvesting part is done by hand. The two leading local wines you should try there are the Cinque Terre DOC, a dry white made with their native Bosco grape combined with Albarola and Vermentino, and the Sciacchetrà DOC (if you are into dessert wines).

Train Hopping

A fast and regular train service connects each of the five Cinque Terre villages. The train is the primary mode of transportation, and if you're only planning to be in Cinque Terre for a day or a couple of days, the train is a must for moving between villages. If you are in Cinque Terre for a few days, plan your base town and a flexible itinerary for the sights you want to see.

Watch the Sunset at Riomaggiore

When the sun is setting in Riomaggiore, many love to go and sit on the rocks at dusk to watch the sunset. Grab your wine or beer and join others as the sun sets for the day. It's a gorgeous, Instagram-worthy shot to watch the day come to an end.

Staying in Cinque Terre

As Cinque Terre is a collection of small villages, you may wonder where to stay for the night (or two).

Riomaggiore

If your base village in Cinque Terre is to stay in Riomaggiore, this is excellent for visitors who love a lively town. (Bonus: It's cheaper here, too!) Some of the places you should consider staying in are

Cà dei Ciuà, Apartments: These apartments are in the center of the village. They have double rooms and bunk beds if you are traveling with kids.
Sottocoperta Guesthouses: This lovely guesthouse offers rooms and apartments, all within a five-minute walk from the village center. The rooms have a fun marine theme; some have balconies and kitchenettes.

Manarola

Manarola is the perfect place for a romantic getaway with its gorgeous views and small streets to stroll along. Here are the top places to stay:

Ca' de' Carlin: These apartments are near Manarola's center. They have a kitchenette, a double bedroom, bunk beds (if you're traveling with kids), and a balcony to view the stunning sites.
Ines Apartments: These apartments are set above Manarola and offer beautiful views of the village. It's also near the train station for your convenience.

Corniglia

If you are looking to stay "off the beaten path," as the saying goes, Corniglia is an excellent option. The best part is that it's not too busy like the other villages, making it much quieter. One thing to keep in mind, however, is Corniglia is only accessible by train, and you'll need to master 377 steps to get into the town (or you can take the bus). Thus, Corniglia is best suited for people who thrive on hiking and those who don't have mobility issues. Here are some of the places you may consider for your stay:

Arbanella: This hotel lets you see stunning town and garden views from your windows and balcony. Each room has air conditioning, a minibar, a fridge, and a coffee machine.

Locanda il Carugio Guesthouse: This hotel offers chic, modern rooms with beautiful sea and mountain views from your balcony! In addition, this hotel provides shared outdoor areas so you can mingle with other guests!

Vernazza

Vernazza is one of the most popular villages because of its streets and colorful houses surrounding the harbor. This is the town that has more restaurants and hotels because it's bigger, so don't be too surprised if trying to find accommodations is challenging. However, here are some great places to stay if you want to stay in Vernazza:

Agriturismo Costa di Campo: This hotel is excellent if you are on a budget and offers full panoramic views of the Cinque Terre from a furnished terrace.

MADA Charm Apartments: The MADA Charm Apartments give you a full mountain view and are steps away from Vernazza Beach!

Monterosso

As Monterosso is the biggest village in Cinque Terre, it's no surprise that it's a popular destination for those who want a beach vacation! What I love about this town is that it contains a modern and older part and historical attractions. So, beach aside, there is a lot to see here! Here are some of the places you should stay at should you decide to stay for a night or two:

La Rosa dei Venti: Set in the heart of the old town, La Rosa dei Venti is a five-minute walk from the beach. Some rooms have a balcony, allowing you to enjoy the views while enjoying your morning coffee.

Affittacamere Monterosso 5 Terre: This hotel is a 15-minute walk from the train station and five minutes from the Ligurian Sea. Each room is quaint, with a staircase to a loft for sleeping!

Albergo Al Carugio: Set in the middle of Monterosso, Albergo Al Carugio is near the train station and has a lovely terrace where you can sit and relax! It's also very close to shops and restaurants!

What NOT to Do in Cinque Terre

Who wouldn't fall in love with this quaint five-village region? The vibrant colors and unique characteristics are enough to make anyone marvel at how gorgeous it is. But, just like visiting Milan (and visiting other places), there are a few things you should avoid doing! Some obvious things you shouldn't do in Cinque Terre include not

- trying to find the perfect village, as each is unique.
- wearing stilettos (stick with the sneakers).
- hoping for a pool.
- hoping to relax on the beaches.
- expecting a lot of shopping opportunities.
- trying to fit everything in, especially if you will only be in Cinque Terre for a day or two.
- forgetting to buy a Cinque Terre card as you need it to use the hiking trails.

Don't Day Trip into Cinque Terre
This tip ties into the last bullet point: Many people try to do all five Cinque Terre villages in one day. Okay, I know we would all love to be world travelers and be able to get to places in a short amount of time, but that is just rushed! You wouldn't even get a lot out of it, to be honest. Consider staying in Cinque Terre for at least three days. That way you can visit each village without rushing through them.

Don't Try Driving in Cinque Terre
Driving in Cinque Terre is an immense pain in the butt and not worth it! It's much faster to take the trains and boat than to drive! Save yourself the headache, and don't bother with driving in this region.

Don't Miss Out on Hiking
You may not be a sporty person, but not taking the time to hike in Cinque Terre can have you missing some gorgeous views and photo-worthy shots!

Cinque Terre is a must-visit destination if you're looking for a breathtaking coastal region to add to your travel list. With five charming villages, a day trip won't be enough to experience all it offers. One of the best ways to see the vibrant colors of this region is by taking a ferry, which will transport you to each village (except for Corniglia). For those who seek a challenge, hiking along the trails is a great option, but remember to get a Cinque Terre card beforehand. Cinque Terre boasts a variety of local eats and wines, so indulge in some of their delicious foods and locally-made wine by making a reservation at a restaurant while you move between the villages. Although this region may be small, it provides a unique perspective on the Italian lifestyle worth experiencing.

While Cinque Terre's way of living is different, given the way it has been formed on the rocky formations, Venice is an entirely different world and one that brings you into a different era altogether.

Chapter 5

Venice—Dos and Don'ts

W ith its many canals, gondolas, and streets that can feel like a maze, Venice (or Venezia) is full of many secrets and mysteries in what is referred to as an island city. It's no wonder it's as romantic as it looks. (Who wouldn't love a romantic boating experience along the canal?)

Beyond the winding streets and canals, Venice has an exciting history and one we won't go too far back into. However, picture this: There were many great triumphs and heartbreaks in the early days, with empires rising and falling, mainly the Roman Empire. Beyond its many challenges and conflicts, Venice became one of the wealthiest regions for importing and trading goods, especially silk, from China. Today, travelers arriving in Venice are not only treated to its stunning architectural designs, but it also makes you feel like you've been transported to another world—the atmosphere is unlike anything else in Italy. (Even Cinque Terre!)

Venice is also where the greeting of "ciao" (pronounced chow) began! It's one of those words that many people know and use like they would "merci" or "bonjour," but weirdly, it had a different meaning than what it is used for today. At one point, ciao was *s'ciao*, which translated and was an abbreviation for declaring yourself to be someone's slave in the Venetian dialect.

As Venice was prominent in trading goods, it was also active in the slave trade. While it essentially would declare the intention of being the enslaved person for someone, it was also a way to convey that this person would be of service to someone else. Eventually, s'ciao morphed into *schiavo* to mean enslaved person (or service person).

That said, while ciao is used casually in our dialect, it has a different meaning while you are in Italy, and you can't use it as a polite greeting to locals (hilariously). Using ciao to greet someone in a shop or your waiter is informal. You will hear many Italians use the word, but observe their mannerisms: they know one another and are not casual acquaintances! Instead of using ciao, use greetings such as *buongiorno*, *salve* (SAL-veh), or *buona sera* (depending on the time of day).

What to DO in Venice

When you are in Venice, be prepared to be enchanted by its very different way of living! It will be unlike anything you will experience in Milan and Cinque Terre because it only has streets and canals to get around—no cars are allowed near the historic center. (We'll discuss more on the car situation in the *What NOT to Do in Venice* section of this chapter.)

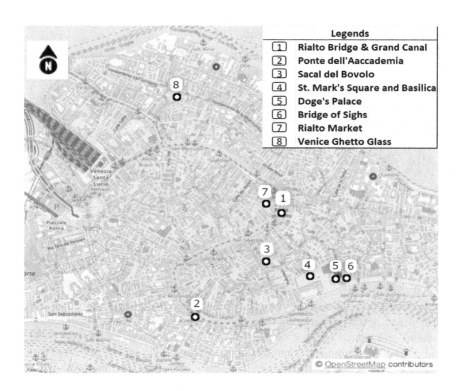

Legends

1. Rialto Bridge & Grand Canal
2. Ponte dell'Aaccademia
3. Sacal del Bovolo
4. St. Mark's Square and Basilica
5. Doge's Palace
6. Bridge of Sighs
7. Rialto Market
8. Venice Ghetto Glass

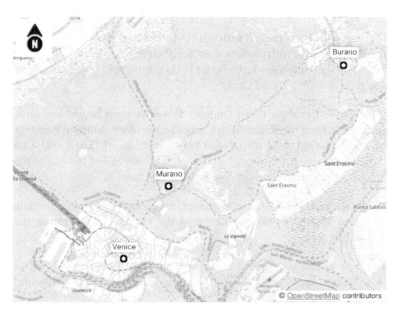

Rialto Bridge and Grand Canal

The Rialto Bridge is the oldest bridge in Venice and is one of the four bridges that connect the land over the Grand Canal. This bridge was once built of wood, but in

the 16th century (the early 1500s), there was talk of replacing it as it had been burned and destroyed on more than one occasion. Interestingly, Michelangelo, Palladio, and Sansovino were all rejected as the architects to replace the wooden bridge. Instead, Antonio da Ponte, a famous Venetian engineer, was entrusted with rebuilding the bridge to what it is today, with construction starting in 1588 and completed in 1591. At the time of its construction, the bridge was the only one to connect the two sides of the Grand Canal until 1854.

The beautiful stone bridge is packed with street vendors and shops—during peak season, expect it to be filled with tourists shopping there! Therefore, if you want to view and marvel at da Ponte's work, it's better to do it from below while watching the gondolas glide along the Grand Canal!

Peaking of the Grand Canal (or Canal Grande), this is Venice's largest and most famous canal! Aside from the Rialto Bridge, you can see other stunning Venetian architecture and get an authentic feel of what Venice is all about! The Grand Canal is one of the main waterways through Venice, splitting one half of the city to the other. It's about 2.5 miles long and has four bridges that cross it.

As the sidewalks are relatively slim to nonexistent, it's a good idea to take a gondola or tourist boat to get the whole experience of the Grand Canal and see the surroundings of this area.

One thing to note is that you should invest in a public transportation ticket in Venice as it will allow you to hop on and off boats as often as you would like and save you money in water taxi fees!

Ponte dell'Accademia

The Ponte dell'Accademia (Accademia Bridge) is another of the four bridges

spanning the Grand Canal built in 1854. This bridge is located at the island's south end and links the Accademia gallery in Dorsoduro to the San Marco district. While its claim to fame is that the bridge is the only one of its kind along this stretch made from timber, the pictures are postcard-worthy! You can view the canal on either side and the Accademia Vaporetto station from the bridge.

If you happen upon some vendors, please know that it is illegal for them to sell goods on this bridge—not only will they get fined, but so will you if you purchase anything from them and get caught in the act!

Scala Contarini del Bovolo

Scala Contarini del Bovolo is a secret, shh! I'm kidding. But the staircase is hidden

in the middle of Venice, and not many tourists know about the 91-foot spiraling staircase that curls up the tower. However, when you climb the 80 monolithic steps to the top, you'll be awarded panoramic views of Venice!

This staircase is a part of the late-Gothic century palace, Palazzo Contarini del Bovolo, built between 1300 and 1400 for the Contarini family. However, the stairs were not added to the palace until the late 15th century. The climb is worth the look, and you should take advantage of it! However, there are some restrictions during the day and peak season, and you must purchase tickets ahead of time. Tickets start at €9.

St. Mark's Square

Going to St. Mark's Square (Piazza San Marco) should be one of the places you should visit in Venice. This square was dedicated to the Evangelist, Mark, who was the patron saint of Venice and is home to many of the important buildings of Venice, including the Clock Tower of Venice (Torre dell Orologio), which displays the time and the dominant Zodiac sign, St. Mark's Basilica (Basilica di San Marco) and Campanile and Doge's Palace.

St. Mark's Basilica

Admission fee: €16

St. Mark's Basilica is Venice's cathedral, which dates back to the ninth century. It

was the original chapel of Doge's Palace next door. However, St. Mark's became Venice's sole cathedral early in the 19th century.The basilica's architecture is stunning, with marble columns, arched portals, and raised cupolas. Inside, you will see over 85,000 square feet of mosaics completed over eight centuries.

If your itinerary has room, check out the museum and terrace overlooking the square because it is a neat perspective!

That said, dress modestly if you enter the church (meaning your knees and shoulders must be covered).

Doge's Palace

Admission fee: from €30

Doge's Palace (Palazzo Ducale) is another must-see in St. Mark's Square. This

palace is another Gothic design constructed between 1309 and 1424 as a fort but was later transformed into a palace. Today, it is a museum with much to admire, including its pink Verona marble, beautiful stone arches, and sculptures! You can also visit a former medieval prison's cells here and stroll over the Bridge of Sighs.

Bridge of Sighs

The Bridge of Sighs (Ponte dei Sospiri) connects the inquisitor's office in Doge's

Palace to the "new" prisons. It earned its name as many 18th-century prisoners would sigh as they took their final glance at the city before being put away for their crimes and losing their lives. It sounds gloomy, but the bridge is gorgeous with its white limestone. You can access this area with a ticket to Doge's palace. Together, that admission starts from €69.

Rialto Market

Venice will give you a stunning backdrop—there's no doubt about that! But markets, where you can purchase fresh fruits, vegetables, and fish, are where the action happens.

The Rialto Market is one of the biggest markets where you can buy fresh fruits and vegetables and is open daily (except for Sundays). This market is an excellent way to immerse yourself in Venice's vibrant life, especially on Saturdays when locals set out to buy fresh produce for their groceries. Although the market is open from 8 a.m. to 4 p.m., the best time to experience the market is between 7:30 a.m. and 9:30 a.m.

Venice Ghetto Glass

The word "ghetto" doesn't have the best connotation attached to it as it's used to describe not-so-great areas; in Central Europe during the Nazi era, the Ghetto was associated with the persecution of Jews and the modern urban slums.

However, way before the era of the Nazis and world wars, the Jews arrived in Venice in the year 1000, and in 1516, a neighborhood was created for the Jews. The intention was not to persecute the Jews but to segregate them from the Roman Catholic Church. In many ways, it was a protected area for the Jewish residents of Venice: During the day, they were free to roam Venice and go to work; at night, the gates were locked, and guards paid by the Jewish community protected the Ghetto. It was a crowded space but home to many.

Much of the world has changed since it was first created, especially during the Second World War. However, it's been reborn recently and is home to around 30 Jewish residents today. As a traveler, you can tour the Ghetto all year at the Museo Ebraico (Jewish Museum) in the Campo Ghetto Nuovo. There, you can see an extensive collection of silverware and religious objects. In addition, the tour will bring you to three synagogues if you are interested in another side of Venetian history and learning about Jewish culture. However, it should be noted that while writing this book, the Venice Ghetto Glass is temporarily closed, so depending on when you are going to Italy, you'll want to search to see when it will reopen and what the hours and admission fees are.

Murano, Burano, and Torcello

Murano, Burano, and Torcello are the three famous islands in Venice's Lagoon, each with its unique appeal:

- Murano's history with creating glassware.
- Burano has stunning lacework and colorful homes.

- Tocello is the Lagoon's first settlement, dating back to the fifth century.

Let's start with Murano and its glasswork. Murano is on the northeast side of Venice and has seven islands, split between canals and connected by the following bridges: Isola dei Conventi, San Donato, Navagero, San Pietro, San Stefano, Sacca Serenella, and Sacca Mattia

Regarding its famous glasswork: In 1291, the Republic of Venice decided that all glasswork workshops would be moved to Murano to contain any adverse outcomes that would follow a disastrous fire from the furnaces.

As for Burano, many visitors marvel at the colors. They remind me of Cinque Terre (but with more intricate designs). However, wandering around this area, you may see some older ladies working away on their laces while chatting with their friends. It's adorable and charming!

As for Torcello, this is the spot where Venice began! It is peaceful, but some attractions are worth checking out, including the cathedral, Basilica di Santa Maria Assunta, and the archaeological museum with old council chambers.

Several guided tours will take you through these islands. Most include a tour through the Murano Glass Factory, where you can see the glass blowers creating several glass pieces, tours of the lace shops in Burano, where you can learn how lace is made, and in Torcello, you can see the oldest mosaics in the Santa Maria Assunta. On one special note, the entry fee into the Santa Maria Assunta is €5 and an additional €4 if you want to climb the bell tower.

Things to Experience and Enjoy in Venice

With so many things to see in Venice, don't forget to experience things too! Being able to experience something like a local is part of the adventure!

Get Lost in Venice

Getting lost in a foreign country seems like the strangest suggestion for someone to experience, but I promise you, it's worth it!

You'll realize that, despite a maze of canals, streets, and bridges, the city is small, so you can get from one end to the other in an hour! But, because it's a slight maze, it's also easy to get lost. However, have you ever found that sometimes getting lost while wandering can be a happy accident? Just think of some of the things you might not have noticed or seen if you stuck to going from point A to point B! You'll be rewarded with some picturesque side streets, hidden cafes, and some craft shops. My advice is to forget the clock while you are in Venice. Let your inner explorer guide you instead!

Venetian Mask-Making Workshop

Venice has a famous carnival called The Carnevale di Venezia. The origins of this carnival are ancient, but it brings tourists annually to admire the costumes and masks parading around the city center. Creating masks is a traditional art in Venice, and it's a unique experience to try out! At the Mask Shop (La Bauta), you can make your mask at a workshop, allowing you to create your own from 50 different models! It's a neat experience and a fantastic way to dive into this cultural tradition!

The Tour of the Bacaro

A *bacaro* is a Venetian tavern with simple wooden furnishings where you can enjoy a glass of wine or spritz and a *cicheti* with small snacks.

On a bacaro tour, you go from one bacaro to the next, enjoying wine or a spritz in different taverns and enjoying the snacks at each stop. It's an inexpensive tour ranging between 0.60 cents to €2 for wine and one and three euros for the cicheti.

Teatro La Fenice

Teatro La Fenice (Phoenix Theater) is Venice's most famous and largest opera theater. It opened in 1792, and on this stage, famous Italian composers debuted their operas, such as Giuseppe Verdi, Vincenzo Bellini, and Gioachino Rossini.

Whether you intend to attend an opera performance or not, it's a stunning place to visit. You'll find a stunning blue ceiling and gold trim inside the opera house. Outside, the building is what you would expect of a traditional Italian villa architecture with white marble and columns.

If you intend to go to a performance, ensure you are appropriately dressed: Men must wear a tuxedo or dark suit with a black tie, and women must wear an evening dress. Your best bet is to check their website to verify the dress code, as it varies for opening night and during the season.

That said, if you want to visit the facility's interior outside of performance times, the opera house is typically open for visits between 9:30 a.m. and 6:00 p.m. You'll need to choose if you will go in the morning or afternoon. Of course, it's subject to change if there are afternoon performances. Pricing is unavailable online, so you must email the info or booking office for tour information.

Dining on the bank of a canal

Dining near a canal in Venice offers a charming and romantic experience. Enjoy traditional Venetian cuisine while soaking up the picturesque views. Indulge in fresh seafood, sip local wines, and savor the ambiance of the gondolas passing by.

It's a truly memorable way to immerse yourself in the magic of Venice. There are several delectable seafood dishes that you should try. Here are the top three seafood dishes to sample in Venice,

Sarde in Saor (Sweet and Sour Sardines): Sarde in Saor is a traditional Venetian dish that combines sardines with sweet and sour flavors. The sardines are first marinated in a mixture of vinegar, onions, raisins, and pine nuts. The combination of sweet and tangy flavors creates a unique taste experience. It is often served as a cicchetti (small snack) in local bars or as an appetizer in restaurants.

Fritto Misto (Mixed Fried Seafood): Fritto Misto is a classic Italian seafood dish that is particularly popular in Venice due to its proximity to the sea. It features a mix of lightly battered and fried seafood, typically including shrimp, squid, scallops, and small fish. The seafood is fried to a golden crispness, resulting in a flavorful and satisfying dish. Fritto Misto is often served with a side of lemon wedges and may be enjoyed as a main course or shared as an appetizer.

Risotto di Gò (Goby Fish Risotto): Risotto di Gò is a traditional Venetian risotto

made with goby fish, a small local fish found in the lagoon of Venice. The fish is simmered with onions, garlic, white wine, and fish broth to create a rich and flavorful base. The rice is then added and cooked until it reaches a creamy consistency. The result is a delicate and aromatic risotto that highlights the flavors of the sea.

A Gondola Ride

It wouldn't feel like an authentic stay in Venice if you didn't take a ride on

a gondola through the canals! Gondolas wait for visitors at every bridge in Venice. Yes, it may seem cliché, but it's a typical Venice thing you'll regret if you skip out.

Before Venice became a world-renowned city for tourists, gondolas were the primary transportation mode. However, with technology and the ability for larger boats, it's taken over some of that tradition—but in hindsight, it fulfills a traveler's romantic dreams by taking in the sights on a calm, smooth ride.

Gondola rides all charge the same price but takes different routes depending on where you begin. You don't want to miss the Grand Canal, which will allow you to go under famous bridges! The standard cost for taking a gondola is €80 for a 25 to 30-minute tour. However, if you're going at night, it's €120 for the same amount of time.

Staying in Venice

Venice has many places you can stay in that suit your needs. What are you looking for? Do you want local charm? Artistic inspiration? Maybe you're looking for luxury indulgence or something that is calming. We'll look at some of the top places you can stay in so that it meets what you are looking for and your budget!

Dorsoduro

We will start with the more budget-friendly areas to stay in. Dorosduro has an artistic heritage, and it's also the area where university students live, so it's a little cheaper, less touristy, and provides an exciting vibe at night. This neighborhood has lovely streets lined with bookshops, cafes, and art galleries. Here are some places to stay:

Sina Centurion Palace: This hotel is a little pricier as it offers five-star luxury service and overlooks the Grand Canal.

The Charming House DD724: If you're looking for something more cost-friendly, check out The Charming House DD724. This hotel is steps away from major attractions and features various works of photography and art collections.

San Marco

The San Marco area is more upscale and luxurious than Dorosduro. It's close to St. Mark's Square and offers luxury shopping options, high-end restaurants, and great views of the Canals.

Baglioni Hotel Luna: The Baglioni Hotel Luna is right along the Grand Canal. From its terraces, you can see some stunning views of Venice!

Hotel Le Isole: The Hotel Le Isole is set in a restored 16th-century building two minutes from St. Mark's Square. If you're on a budget, this is the hotel you should consider looking into!

Cannaregio

The Cannaregio neighborhood is on the north side of Venice. It's the second-largest district with several historic sights and unique landmarks. Like the Dorsoduro neighborhood, Cannaregio is an excellent area to stay in if you're sticking to a tighter budget. Some places to stay are

Alle Guglie Boutique Hotel: The Alle Guglie Boutique Hotel is in a renovated historic building set in a lovely area with markets and shops. It's a 10-minute walk from St. Mark's Square and the Rialto Bridge.

Foscari Palace: The Foscari Palace is an interesting hotel dating back to the 1500s! (So, you're literally stepping back in time by staying here!) But don't worry. You won't be living in the 1500s at this hotel—it's been refurbished but still has its original elegance. This hotel overlooks the Grand Canal and is five minutes from the Rialto Bridge.

Santa Croce and San Polo

The Santa Croce and San Polo neighborhoods are excellent if you want to immerse yourself among the locals and their way of living in Venice. These areas have a genuine charm with small squares, slim alleys, and busy markets. These neighborhoods also have several trattorias and bacaros to enjoy Venetian cuisine and wines.

In addition, Santa Croce is one of Venice's main transportation hubs and can give you that "off-the-beaten-path" feel! Here are the places you should stay:

Residenza d'Epoca San Cassiano: The Residenza d'Epoca San Cassiano is a 14th-century villa with a true feel to it! This hotel has antiques and Murano glass chandeliers with no modernization! It's a unique hotel to stay in!

Albergo Marin: The Albergo Marin hotel is family-run and is close to the Lucia Train Station and Grand Canal. In addition, it has a kitchenette so you can prepare some of your meals!

Ca' San Polo: The Ca' San Polo hotel is set in a 15th-century building but was renovated in 2003. A terrace offers a stunning panoramic view of the San Polo district and is very close to the Rialto Bridge and San Marco Square.

Central Castello

Castello is another large region in Venice, just east of San Marco, and extends from the Rialto Bridge and town center to the Giardi Gardens and Arsenale Naval Base. It's much quieter here, but you can expect to find small squares and local shops to suit your needs. As for hotels, here are some of the best options:

Hotel Bucintoro: The Hotel Bucintoro is right along the waterfront and neighbors the San Biagio Church. You can enjoy a panoramic view over the Venice Lagoon from the rooms.

Hotel Le Isole: The Hotel Le Isole is a budget-friendly boutique hotel furnished with original paintings and wooden floors in a restored 16th-century building. Guests say that the concierge service is knowledgeable and available 24 hours daily.

Eastern Castello

Eastern Castello gives you a quieter retreat away from the hustle and bustle of Venice, especially during tourist season. You can expect a more tranquil atmosphere and the chance to experience the Venetian way of life with it being less crowded. Some places you may want to consider staying in include

La Residenza: Once the home of the Gritti noble family, the La Residenza is set in a 15th-century building behind the Church of San Giovanni and along the waterfront. The ensuite rooms are furnished with 18th-century Venetian décor.

Palazzo Soderini: The Palazzo Soderini is set in the center of Venice and is 10 minutes from St. Mark's Square. The building dates back to the 18th century, and you'll find that the rooms have a minimalist design.

Mestre

The Mestre district, dating back to the 13th century, is located near Venice and is connected to the mainland by the Liberty Bridge. By staying here, you're likely to save some money since it's not directly connected to the hustle and bustle of Venice. From this district, you can have a birds-eye view of Venice and its lagoon, but you can also visit some areas not covered in this chapter, such as 1) Piazza Ferretto, which has several sightseeing, shopping, and dining options, 2) San Giuliano Park, where you can pack a picnic, hike, and watch a local concert and , 3) Duomo di Mestre (also known as the Church of San Lorenzo) is well-known for its limestone.

Some places to stay are

Hotel Al Vivit: The Hotel Al Vivit is a renovated 18th-century building in the Piazza Ferretto. It's near a bus stop that will take you to Venice. If you go during the summer, enjoy a lovely buffet breakfast on the terrace before you set out on your adventures for the day!

Leonardo Royal Hotel Venice Mestre: This four-star hotel is close to the Piazza Ferretto and 10 minutes from Venice's city center.

Noale

Noale is a small medieval town located 30 minutes outside of Venice. Some people think of this area as a scene out of *Game of Thrones*, as its roots go back to the Iron Age. As it's outside of Venice, you can have a different journey as you stroll around the Gothic streets and admire the Padua Tower on the west side of the town. Some places to stay in Noale include

Residence Le Bugne: This hotel is 9.32 miles from the Mestre Ospedale Train Station. It has a garden in which you can sit, a fully equipped kitchenette if you want to cook some of your food and a hot tub.

Hotel Due Torri Tempesta: The Hotel Due Torri Tempesta is a family-owned hotel featuring 40 rooms with a contemporary design. If you want to venture into Venice from this hotel, a bus service is outside the hotel doors.

What NOT to Do in Venice

Venice is a hot spot for tourists, especially during the summer months. As a result, it can cause some friction if you do some things that are otherwise frowned upon.

Don't Expect to Drive in Venice

Venice does have cars, but they're not permitted in the city's center. When you arrive in Venice, you will notice that it is a town where everyone walks (or takes the gondolas). If you rent a car for a road trip around the country, you can park outside the city's center.

Don't Swim in Canals

Yes, the water may be inviting (especially if you go during the summer months). Still, the canals are considered public roads, and the chances of you getting hit by the propeller of a passing taxi or gondola paddle are pretty high. You'll also get hit with a hefty fine. Save the dip in the water for the beach!

Don't forget to validate your vaporetto ticket.

If you're using public transportation boats (vaporetto), ensure that you validate your ticket at the ticket machines before boarding. Failure to do so may result in fines if the ticket inspectors check you.

Don't ignore the "No Photography" signs

Some churches, museums, and galleries in Venice may have restrictions on photography. Respect these rules and refrain from taking photos where it is prohibited. Always be mindful of the privacy and sanctity of religious spaces.

Don't Sit in the Alleys or on Bridges

Since Venice is a walking town, sitting on the bridges in the narrow alleyways can cause an interruption to the foot traffic. It's almost like stopping your car in the middle of four-lane traffic. Find a field with more public space instead of sitting in the alleys or bridges. If you must stop, keep to the right (especially when passing through narrower areas).

As Venice is historic for many reasons, it's no wonder that thousands of people travel to the city every year! Many charming and iconic landmarks include the Grand Canal, Rialto Bridge, and Gondola rides! Venice is one of those cities you can easily get lost in (and you should) to get a taste of their life and traditions.

Venice is full of life, but Tuscany has a significant artistic and cultural heritage, many natural reserves, and stunning landscapes to marvel at!

Chapter 6

Tuscany—Dos and Don'ts

Tuscany (*Toscana*) is a west-central Italy region along the Ligurian and Tyrrhenian seas. When people hear Tuscany, many (myself included) may often think about the 2003 movie *Under the Tuscan Sun* starring Diane Lane, whose character impulsively bought a villa in Tuscany to change her life (Wells, 2003). More interesting is that the film is based on a book of the same name written by Frances Mayes, first published in 1996. The film and book both bring viewers and readers stunning imagery of Tuscany, but once you walk the streets to explore it, you will truly know what it's like to live under the stunning sun.

That said, despite the whimsical life that Tuscany brings, it was home to many famous names in the world of music, literature, and science. These names included Leonardo da Vinci, Galilei Puccini, Michelangelo, Sandro Botticelli, Brunelleschi, Dante Alighieri, Giotto, Boccaccio, and Lorenzo de Medici.

As for literature, *The Adventures of Pinocchio*, written by Collodi and first published in 1883 (and later translated to English), captured the hearts of many Italian children. For those who don't know much about Pinocchio, it's about a puppet who dreams of becoming a real boy but winds up in some mishaps. Collodi's upbringing in Tuscany inspired the story, and there are many tributes to him in that region today!

Tuscany will steal your heart with its unique landscapes, art, and history. It has a one-of-a-kind natural and cultural heritage that many travelers have enjoyed over the years. Let's explore some things you should do, see, and experience while exploring Tuscany.

What to DO in Tuscany

The history of Tuscany dates back more than 3,000 years ago and has many things to see, do, and experience. Even so, it's a region in Italy where romance and relaxation come with these adventures and experiences, creating the ultimate vacation. Tuscany's buildings and monuments were built with stone, marble, and terracotta, all still standing today. Consider including some of these spots when planning your trip to this region!

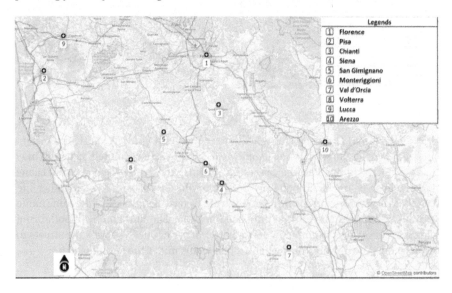

Legends

1. Florence
2. Pisa
3. Chianti
4. Siena
5. San Gimignano
6. Monteriggioni
7. Val d'Orcia
8. Volterra
9. Lucca
10. Arezzo

© OpenStreetMap contributors

Florence

Florence (*Firenze*) is the capital city of Tuscany and the most visited area of this

region. Founded in 59 B.C.E. by Emperor Julius Caesar, Florence was once home to a large Roman army camp. Today, however, Florence embodies so much more in its history, including symbolizing the Renaissance period. Here are some places you should consider checking out while in Florence, Tuscany.

The Palazzo Vecchio

The Palazzo Vecchio was once Florence's main palace owned by the Medicis, but today it is a government building. However, it does have a museum, and you can go up the spire to enjoy a panoramic view of Florence. Tickets to enter the Palazzo Vecchio are €10 if the visitors are between 0 and 17 years old and €12,50 for 18 and up. (Bonus tip: If you pick up a Firenze card, it's free!)

The Pitti Palace and Boboli Gardens

The Pitti Palace and Boboli Gardens have a fascinating (somewhat funny) history: The palace's construction began in 1457 by Luca Pitti and was meant to overshadow the Medicis' palace. Unfortunately, the Pittis could no longer afford the construction and relinquished it to the Medicis in 1549. Regardless of ownership (which changed again in subsequent years), its stunning interior remains. Outside, the Boboli Gardens offer stunning sculptures and views of the Tuscany countryside. Tickets to enter the palace are from €16; the garden costs €11,20.

Florentine Churches

Check out some of the Florentine churches, including Santa Maria del Fiore, the Florence Cathedral, the Santa Croce, and the Santa Maria's Novella. Remember that if you are visiting a church, be appropriately dressed, including no bare shoulders, covered knees, and closed-toe shoes (no sandals). Here are the costs to get into each:

Church	Hours of operation	Cost
Santa Maria del Fiore and the Florence Cathedral	Monday to Saturday from 10:15 a.m. to 4:15 a.m.	Free admission unless you want to climb the Brunelleschi Dome. The dome cost is €35 for adults and €20 for visitors between 7 and 14 years old. If you plan to visit the dome, you must book your tickets in advance.
	This church is closed on Sundays and public holidays.	
Santa Maria Novella	Monday to Saturday from 10 a.m. to 5 p.m. and Sunday from 1 p.m. to 5 p.m.	Adults: €7,50
		Children between 12 and 18 years old: €5
		Children between 0 and 11 years old are free.
Santa Croce	Monday and Wednesday to Saturday from 9:30 a.m. to 5:30 p.m.	Adults: €9
	Sundays from 1 p.m. to 5:30 p.m.	Children between 12 and 17 years old: €7
	Closed on Tuesdays	Children between 0 and 11 years old are free.

Pisa

The Leaning Tower of Pisa is primarily the landmark people think of when they

hear Pisa, but this region has a lot more to it. (And you should explore Pisa beyond the city center—but more on that part later!)

Piazza delle Vettovaglie

The Piazza delle Vettoaglie is one square you'll want to explore while in Pisa as it becomes a morning market filled with local fruits, vegetables, and other food products. It's a fun way to see how the Tuscans live and interact with one another! However, this square is also surrounded by other local shops, cafes, and wine bars, an excellent spot for an appetizer or mid-day snack!

Arsenali Medicei Pisa (Historical Ships Museum in Pisa)

This museum is excellent if you are traveling with kids! It displays seven Roman-era ships dating back from the third to the seventh century B.C.E. and over 8,000 artifacts. The museum is open between 10 a.m. and 4 p.m. on Tuesday, Wednesday, and Thursday and from 10 a.m. to 1 p.m. on Fridays. The full price of admission is €10; however, there are some other pricing points to be aware of:

Free	Reduced €8	Reduced €5	Family ticket €20
Children up to 6 years old	Groups of 10 or more	Visitors between 6 and 18 can visit the museum at a reduced rate of €5.	Families with two adults and three children between 6 and 18 years old can enter the museum for €20.
Visitors with disabilities and support	People who are 65 and up		
Tour guides and their leaders			

Please note that the museum is closed on Mondays, December 25, January 1, Easter Sunday, and August 15.

Chianti

Chianti (pronounced kee-yaan-tee) is one of Tuscany's most stunning and well-known regions. With its luscious rolling green hills extending between Florence and Siena, Chianti is rich with history, especially regarding wine! This region is the ultimate romantic getaway for those wanting to experience another medieval village setting, as it features castles, farms, and various wineries along the way. But aside from wine, there are several other spots you should check out!

Montefioralle

Montefioralle is a small, picturesque village with a former castle on a steep hill overlooking Chianti, with several stone buildings and a couple of restaurants. As it is a small town, public transportation doesn't stop here. However, you can access the town by foot if you are willing to brave a hike up a 1.24-mile steep hill or by car.

San Casciano in Val di Pesa

San Casciano is one of the entry points into Chianti and is very close to Florence, making it a perfect day trip! What is great about this little town is that it's not overrun with tourists, making it more enjoyable to wander around. You can find some lovely trattorias, the Sacred Art Museum, and other nice shops in this area. The best way to get to San Casciano is by car; however, there is a direct bus from Florence.

Volpaia

The tiny village of Volpaia is stunning with its ancient stone walls, doorways, and climbing flowers. It was once another castle in the area and today serves as an informal spot to enjoy wine in the Medieval tower. In addition, you can enjoy some delicious foods at small eateries or restaurants that overlook the vineyards. The best way to get to Volpaia is by car as there is no public transportation.

Castelnuovo Berardenga

Castelnuovo Berardenga is in the south part of Chianti, encompassing a few villas and an enchanting landscape. In this region, you can visit some of the parish churches and enjoy the slower-paced life of this area. The best way to access Castelnuovo is by car; however, there is also a direct bus from Siena.

Siena

Many people who have traveled through Tuscany say that Siena is one of their favorites in the region for its unique and preserved medieval buildings dating back to the 1300s. This region goes as far back as the Etruscan era (roughly ca. 900 to 500 B.C.E.) but was firmly established in the Medieval period as a rival against Florence.

While in Siena, you should check out

- the Duomo di Siena for its stunning Gothic exterior and mosaic-decorated floor.
- the top of the Torre del Mangia. (The 400 steps to the top are worth it for the countryside view!)
- the market, which happens every Wednesday between 8:30 a.m. and 1:30 p.m.

San Gimignano

Like Siena, travelers are drawn to San Gimignano for its enchanting setting,

including its squares, shops, and frescoes.

San Gimignano is halfway between Siena and Florence and feels like you have stepped back in time the moment you step through its gates with its old stone buildings and 14 tower houses. You can explore areas such as the Tore Grossa, where you climb 214 steps to see a picturesque view of the city, and if you're not squeamish, the Museum of Torture is one for the thrill of viewing Medieval torture. (You may wince, but if you're traveling with teens, it may entertain them.)

Val d'Orcia

Val d'Orcia delivers stunning rolling green hills with a lone cypress on the skyline. This gorgeous landscape is one of the most picturesque parts of Tuscany and one that many Renaissance artists like Sandro Botticelli loved to paint.

This region is well-known for its wine and food, including the pecorino cheese of Pienza. While in Val d'Orcia, check out the Chapel of Madonna di Vitaleta!

Volterra

Volterra is a village on top of a cliff that you can see from afar. It's surrounded by

double walls from the Etruscan and 13th centuries, giving off a medieval vibe in addition to it being a historic village.

As you wander around Volterra's streets, don't forget to check out the Roman Theater that dates back to the first century. Interestingly, this theater was not discovered until the 1950s—it served as a dump for years that hid it. A few museums in Volterra also showcase raw artifacts crafted by the Etruscans and Romans.

Lucca

Another beloved artistic region, Lucca, is known for its many churches, which

earned its rightful nickname of "the city of a hundred churches." While wandering the streets of Luca, you can check out the many cathedrals, but there are many ceramic shops, too! Some tours available in Lucca include a glass-blowing tour, a walking tour, and food tasting. However, this is one of those regions where you should walk around and explore alone!

Arezzo

Located an hour southeast of Florence, Arezzo is a small town easily reachable by

train. It's an ideal place to spend a day and see the major sights without being overcrowded by tourists. Some places to do and see while in Arezzo include

- Church of San Francesco
- Piazza Grande (the main square)
- Casa Vasari, where Italian Mannerist artist, Giorgio Vasari, lived

Things to Experience and Enjoy in Tuscany

The things to experience and enjoy while in Tuscany are unlimited! There are so many landscapes and medieval sites to see it can feel overwhelming to decide what to do. Look no further: I am here to guide you on some things you should experience and enjoy in Tuscany!

Tour Pisa

Visiting Pisa may seem cliché, especially if you take a photo with the Leaning Tower of Pisa as if you are propping it up like many others like to do. Despite having a four-degree lean, it's a beautiful tower to admire with its white marble exterior.

However, several other structures are near and in the city's historic center beyond the tower, including a cathedral, baptistry, and cemetery. So, while checking out Pisa is worth it (especially if it's on your bucket list), don't forget about the other monuments and sites around it!

Go, Truffle Hunting,

Tuscany is a popular spot for truffles and truffle hunting—and no, I'm not referring to those delicious truffle chocolates. Truffles are essentially mushrooms that grow underground in wooded areas. Hunting for these delicious delicacies happens year-round, with assorted truffles to be found over the different seasons. Using truffles in dishes adds a new level of class and some distinctive flavors for everyone to enjoy.

You can try this on your own, but booking a private truffle hunt with a guide may be your best bet to be hunting in the right spots. Your guide will meet you with their truffle hunting dog and give you a lesson before you head out into the oak forests to hunt for truffles for a few hours. Following the truffle hunt, you will go to a local winery and enjoy a relaxing dinner, wine, and olive oils to complement the truffles.

See Renaissance Art in Florence

Fun fact: Did you know that Florence was the birthplace of the Renaissance movement? As Florence is a starting point for some fantastic art history, it's worth it to check out some art galleries, especially the Accademia Gallery, which has the famous "David" statue created by Michelangelo and Botticelli's "Birth of Venus" at the Uffizi Gallery. Some other Renaissance art you should check out include

Lorenzo Ghiberti's The Gates of Paradise: Nicknamed as such by Michelangelo, these bronze doors display Biblical scenes across ten panels. The doors were installed at the Baptistery of San Giovanni in 1452 and can be seen on the eastern entrance.
Bartolomeo Ammannati's Fountain of Neptune: Set right in the middle of Florence's Piazza della Signoria, this fountain was sculpted in the 16th century.
San Marco Museum: The San Marco Museum houses a massive collection of frescoes painted by Fra Angelico, a Dominican monk who saw painting as a form of prayer.

Visit Film Location Sites

If you have seen *Under the Tuscan Sun* or *Quantum of Solace*, you may recognize some places when visiting Tuscany! For travelers who are movie buffs, you may want to take a guided tour that will bring you to several sites from different movies, including

- *The Twilight Saga: New Moon* (2010)
- The new version of *Pinocchio* starring Tom Hanks (2022)
- *Gladiator* (2000)
- *Letters to Juliet* (2010)

Experience Open-Air Art at Il Giardino dei Tarocchi

It's an unusual thing to do in Tuscany, but visit the Il Giardino dei Tarocchi, which translates to *The Tarot Garden* in English. In this garden, you can immerse yourself in the strangest modern art collections created by French artist Niki de Saint Phalle beginning in 1979; it took her nearly 20 years to complete her exciting work with a goal in mind to create a magnificent magical garden. Her sculptures are around 12 to 15 meters high, made of iron, cement, mosaic tiles, glass shards, and old ruins. This park is open between April and mid-October. Here are the prices to enter:

- Regular admission: €14
- Visitors between 7 and 65 years old: €9
- Visitors between 0 and 6 years old are free

Take a Hot Air Balloon Ride

If you're a brave person who likes to take an adventure to the next level, a hot air balloon ride is a great way to see the Tuscan landscape, castles, duomos, and villas from the sky. Rides typically begin at sunrise (but you can book them anytime during the day up to dusk). Some other things to keep in mind are to dress warmly with layers and wear comfortable shoes.

Wine and Olive Oil Tastings

Tuscany is well-known for its wine and olives, so this is one experience you should consider while in this region! If you want to experience touring the wine country in Tuscany, start in Montalcino and try out their famous red wine paired with meat, mushrooms, and truffles. From there, head over to Montepulciano, where you'll be charmed by some Renaissance buildings, churches, and artisan workshops. Here, you should check out the city center's monumental cellars and take a wine tour in the countryside. You will want to try out some Chianti wine in Chianti for your last stop.

Castellina in Chianti is also the place to try olive oil. Many local wineries offer olive oil samples that can be tried during tours.

Cooking Classes in Tuscany

We know that Italians love their food, so taking a cooking class with a local in Tuscany is an excellent way to try making local delicacies, including pasta, pizza, and gelato! In addition, this is another way to sample local wine and learn more about the wine-making processes and how to pair it with your meals.

There are several places in Tuscany where you can join cooking classes and learn the art of Tuscan cuisine. Here are a few popular options:

Cooking schools: Tuscany is home to various cooking schools that offer hands-on classes for both beginners and advanced cooks. Schools such as Apicius

International School of Hospitality and Cordon Bleu Firenze provide professional culinary training and offer short-term courses or one-day workshops for tourists.

Agriturismi: Agriturismi are farm-stays in Tuscany that often offer cooking classes as part of their agritourism experience. These classes provide an opportunity to learn traditional Tuscan recipes using fresh ingredients sourced directly from the farm. Agriturismi like Fattoria Poggio Alloro and Agriturismo La Pieve offers cooking classes in a rustic and authentic setting.

Wineries: Some Tuscany wineries offer cooking classes combining wine tasting with culinary experiences. Participants can learn to pair Tuscan wines with local dishes and gain insights into regional wine production while honing their cooking skills. Wineries like Tenuta Torciano and Castello Banfi offer such classes.

Local Chefs and Restaurants: Many local chefs and restaurants in Tuscany provide cooking classes where you can learn the secrets of Tuscan cuisine from experienced professionals. These classes often include visits to local markets, hands-on cooking sessions, and the chance to enjoy the prepared dishes. Notable options include Cucina Giuseppina and Cooking in Florence.

Culinary Tours: Consider joining a culinary tour in Tuscany, which typically includes cooking classes as part of the itinerary. These tours offer a comprehensive culinary experience, combining visits to local markets, cooking sessions, wine tastings, and dining at renowned Tuscan restaurants. Tour operators such as Walks of Italy and The International Kitchen organize such culinary tours.

When planning to join a cooking class in Tuscany, it's advisable to research and book in advance, considering factors like location, availability, class size, and the specific focus of the class (e.g., pasta making, wine pairing, or regional specialties). This will ensure a delightful and enriching culinary experience in the heart of Tuscany.

While in Tuscany, you must try and savor the region's renowned culinary delights. Here are three must-try dishes that showcase the flavors of Tuscany:

Bistecca alla Fiorentina (Florentine Steak): Bistecca alla Fiorentina is a famous

Tuscan dish that showcases the region's exceptional beef. It consists of a thick-cut T-bone or porterhouse steak, traditionally sourced from the Chianina cattle breed. The steak is grilled over an open flame, seasoned simply with salt, pepper, and olive oil, and cooked to medium-rare perfection. The result is a tender and flavorful steak with a charred exterior. It's typically shared between multiple people due to its size, making it a sociable and indulgent dining experience.

Pappardelle al Cinghiale (Pappardelle with Wild Boar Ragu): Tuscany's rich and hearty cuisine is exemplified by

Pappardelle al Cinghiale. This dish features broad, ribbon-like pasta called pappardelle, served with a slow-cooked ragu made from tender, flavorful wild boar meat. The ragu is typically cooked with aromatic ingredients such as garlic, onions, tomatoes, herbs, and red wine. The combination of the tender pasta and the robust, gamey ragu creates a genuinely satisfying and comforting dish.

Ribollita: Ribollita is a traditional Tuscan soup that has humble origins but bursts

with flavor. It is made by simmering a mixture of cannellini beans, stale bread, kale or other greens, onions, carrots, celery, and tomatoes. The soup is simmered to allow the flavors to meld together, and it's often served with a drizzle of extra-virgin olive oil. Ribollita is a nourishing and rustic dish that showcases Tuscany's focus on simple, quality ingredients.

Bagno Vignoni Hot Springs

Tuscany may be ancient, but it has some spa towns, too. However, Bagno Vignoni is the only spot that offers free spas. It's about an hour South of Siena, and you can use the outdoor sulfur pools for free!

Canyoneering

Canyoneering is an exciting and adventurous experience for anyone ten and older! This adventure is a fun way to see other beautiful sites beyond the ancient medieval buildings. All canyoneering expeditions should be done with a guide for your safety so that you can explore the gorges and canyons within Tuscany.

Staying in Tuscany

Tuscany offers so many picturesque views and things to do in each town that it can feel tricky to decide where to stay. Before continuing, decide what you want to get from your trip to Tuscany, including what areas you'd like to visit and what you want to do.

One of the better options for staying in Tuscany is to rent an Airbnb, as it allows you to shop and live like a local. However, I've got you covered if you wish to stay at a hotel!

Florence

Florence is one of the spots you will want to stay in if you intend to explore as much of Italy's Renaissance history as possible. Here are some of the places you should consider checking out for accommodation:

Hotel Alba Palace: The Hotel Alba Palace is excellent if you're looking for something budget-friendly. It's near the Santa Maria Novella Basilica, and each room is decorated with a traditional style, showcasing some Renaissance prints on the wall.

Palazzo Castri 1874: The Palazzo Castri 1874 is in a 19th-century building with some rooms overlooking a garden outside. It's near the Santa Maria Novella Train Station for public transport convenience and has an outdoor pool for the afternoons if you want to relax.

Siena

Siena has many great sites to check out and things to experience, including its church, Duomo di Siena, and many masterpieces by several Renaissance artists. Several accommodations can meet budget needs, especially if you are backpacking through Italy. Here are some places to stay:

Albergo Chiusarelli: This hotel is a three-star accommodation with rooms that have been renovated to match the neoclassical style. Every room has air conditioning, and some rooms will either overlook a football stadium or the town center. There is no elevator in this hotel.

Palazzo Ravizza: The Palazzo Ravizza is a family-run hotel that has been open since 1922. It offers elegant rooms with furnishings from the 1920s. This hotel also has a garden overlooking the countryside.

Chianti

If you're looking for a region near the wineries, Chianti is where you should stay. As for accommodations, the Chianti Classico has some great places to stay while in Tuscany. Some places you should consider checking out to stay include

Casalta Boutique Hotel: The Casalta Boutique Hotel is a budget-friendly and family-owned set in an old Lombard fortress. Nearby is an outdoor pool, hiking, horse-riding facilities, golfing, and tennis courts.

Borgo San Luigi: Submerged in Tuscany's countryside, the Borgo San Luigi is set in a 17th-century palace, surrounded by stunning gardens and an Olympic-sized pool. This hotel is excellent as the staff can help organize tours for you if you're not sure where you want to start.

Val d'Orcia

Val d'Orcia is one area seen on many Italian postcards due to its gorgeous green and golden landscapes. It does not have many historical sites, but Val d'Orcia has a specific wine road with many vineyards extending between Montepulciano and Montalcino. Most of the hotels in this area are considered classic Tuscan villas with their vineyards and pools, so prices can sometimes run a little high—but I did manage to find some that are budget-friendly, too:

Hotel Rutiliano: The Hotel Rutiliano is a few steps from the historic center and about a 15-minute drive from Montepulciano. This hotel also has a small pool with deck chairs and umbrellas.
Grand Hotel Impero: The Grand Hotel Impero is at the bottom of Mount Amiata. This hotel is excellent if you're looking for a resort, as it has a wellness center on the property offering services such as a relaxation area, a Turkish bath, a sauna, sensory showers, and a hot tub.
Adler Spa Resort Thermae: This hotel is another great one to stay in if you are looking for a resort, as it has over 1,000 square meters of indoor and outdoor swimming pools and panoramic countryside views. This hotel is also kid-friendly as it has a kids' club! Additionally, the Adler Spa Resort Thermae offers free biking and trekking excursions, private tours of wineries, cooking classes, cheese and olive oil tastings, and hot air balloon rides!

Lucca

Lucca is a great spot to stay in if you want to check out several churches! This area has lovely restaurants, cafes, and gelato shops. It's also the base stop for many Tuscan regions, including Florence, Siena, and Pisa, which you can easily reach by car. In addition to some Renaissance-style apartments for rent, you can check out some of these hotel accommodations:

San Marco Holidays: San Marco Holidays is within steps of the city center, and many attractions are visible from the hotel. There is a pool, a private park, and a terrace for your enjoyment.
Hotel Ilaria: The Hotel Ilaria is a renovated historic stable and 14th-century church within Lucca's walls. They have a free bicycle service that will make your Lucca exploration much more effortless and hassle-free!

Arezzo

Arezzo is the place to stay if you love art and shopping! Art lovers love Arezzo for its neat masterpieces throughout the town. People who love shopping love the stalls and the antique market on the first weekend of every month. Here are some places to stay:

iConic B&B Wellness Resort: This resort offers a year-round outdoor pool and is about a 15-minute drive from Piazza Grande. It's also near the Arezzo train station, connecting you to Florence, Borgo San Lorenzo, Lucca, Pisa, Siena, Viareggio, and Grosseto.

Etrusco Arezzo Hotel: The Etrusco Arezzo Hotel offers spacious rooms and is near the fairgrounds and Arezzo's city center.

What NOT to do in Tuscany

With so many things to explore in Tuscany, it's easy to forget what you shouldn't do (even if they are obvious, like not wearing high-heeled shoes). Let's look at what you should avoid doing when in Tuscany.

Avoid Driving in the Bigger Towns
As tempting as it can be to drive everywhere, it can be a bigger pain when you are within the town limits due to poor signage indicating speed changes, among other things related to driving in Tuscany; unfortunately, these driving mishaps can land you with hefty fines making your trip more expensive! It's better to drive between the towns and then park your car at your accommodation for your stay and walk or take public transportation, if available. Otherwise, use the train!

Don't Fill Up Your Whole Schedule
Unless you plan to spend your entire vacation in Tuscany, it's impossible to see everything (even then, if you're there a week or two, you don't see it all). Remember to pick and choose what you want to do and see and build your plan around that. But also, be open to getting lost in the countryside and exploring the intricate medieval towns. Lastly, leave some space to relax, especially if you stay in a hotel with a pool!

Don't Wear Flip-Flops
While wearing high heels should be a definite no-no due to the cobblestones and narrow walkways, flip-flops should also go on the list of items you shouldn't wear around Tuscany. You'll stand out as a tourist. Additionally, remember that open-toed shoes are prohibited in churches.

Don't Wait in Line
You can book your tickets in advance for most attractions, especially in peak months! Book your tickets online to save yourself the pain of wasting time in line. If the option is available for a time stamp, I'd highly recommend picking the time you want to go!

Don't Assume Museums and Galleries Are Family-Friendly
Some museums, such as the Palazzo Vecchio, are family-friendly, but not all are. It's best to plan when visiting museums and galleries to see which ones may be more family-friendly, and pick a few works you want to see as a family before heading outside.

Don't Just Visit the Leaning Tower of Pisa

When anyone hears Pisa, it's natural that they'll immediately picture the famous monument. Realistically, if the Leaning Tower of Pisa wasn't in Pisa, I think this town would not be on someone's list of places to see in Italy. While taking that famous photo of you propping the tower up is fun, take the time to go beyond the Leaning Tower of Pisa! Beyond the Campo dei Miracoli Square, where the tower is, you will find that Pisa is a university city and has a beautiful river promenade to see and walk along. Take the time to explore other areas in Pisa because there is much more to uncover!

Don't ignore local wine traditions

Tuscany is renowned for its wine production, especially its famous red wine, Chianti. When visiting wineries or wine bars, respect the local wine traditions. Take the time to savor the flavors and aromas of the wines and engage in conversations about the wine culture.

Don't expect late-night dining

Unlike some other regions in Italy, Tuscany generally follows traditional dining hours. Many restaurants close for a break between lunch and dinner service. Plan your meals accordingly, and be aware that late-night dining options may be limited.

Don't pick wildflowers or plants

Tuscany's countryside is known for its beauty and diverse flora. Avoid picking wildflowers or plants as they disrupt the natural environment and may violate local regulations.

Tuscany is a stunning region to visit, especially if you enjoy Renaissance masterpieces, wine, olive oil, and cheese! While traveling through the beautiful countryside, be sure to take the time to explore some of the medieval spots (as there are plenty of them) in addition to the big attractions, such as the Leaning Tower of Pisa! However, Tuscany can be about more than just the typical attractions and sites; you can also take the time to go on adventures such as canyoneering or soaking up in some hot springs. There is plenty to do in Tuscany, but ensure you decide what you want to see and do because time is of the essence, and you can't fit everything in realistically.

Tuscany is one of the more memorable places to go to. However, Rome is another stunning city in Italy that should be on your Italian traveling list, especially with its historical monuments that helped to shape this significant city.

Chapter 7

Rome—Dos and Don'ts

T he ancient city of Rome (*Roma*), also known as the "Eternal City," brims with so much rich history, beauty, and wonder; as a result, it should come as no surprise that Rome is one of the more popular Italian destinations travelers venture to yearly. Here are some quick facts about Rome before we dive into everything you should (and should *not*) do:

- Rome has more than 900 churches and 280 fountains. Can you guess which church is the largest one? The St. Peter's Basilica inside Vatican City!
- If you're a pasta lover, Rome has a museum dedicated to this beloved dish! It's called The Pasta Museum of Rome (or Il Museo della Pasta di Roma).
- Nearly 700,000 euros (over $775,000) worth of coins are thrown into the Trevi Fountain annually. The coins are collected and donated to charities.
- La Sapienza was Rome's first university, established in 1303. It remains the largest university in Europe and the second largest globally.
- A law in Rome allows cats to roam freely. Protecting cats in Rome has been a tradition since the ancient days as they were sacred animals to the goddess Diana. They were also a way to maintain rodents throughout the city.

Walking through Rome is literally a historical walk, all thanks to its massive artistic and architectural heritage. Rome's enchanting city has been captured beautifully over centuries by artists and poets alike. It's also why so many people wish to return and throw their coins into the Trevi Fountain because it has captured their souls in a way that no other trip has. Rome is everything we all imagine and more— the first time, the second time, and beyond that.

As people hear the word Pisa and immediately picture the Leaning Tower, people often envision Rome's Colosseum, the Trevi Fountain, and St. Peter's Basilica. There are many more fountains and churches (as you learned in the quick facts) and several monuments beyond the famous Colosseum. And, despite its architecture lining the streets, it's one of the greener cities in Europe, surrounded by parks and gardens. Be prepared to have your breath taken away when you visit Rome.

What to DO in Rome

There is no shortage of things to do and experience in the ancient city of Rome! Of course, the number of things you can see and do can feel overwhelming. Remember that just as Rome was not built in a day, your exploration of the ancient city will also not happen in a day. Even then, you won't be able to see everything in a few days. (But that's what becoming a traveler is for!) Whether you're in Rome for a couple of days, a week, or a couple of weeks, there are many things to see and do. From this section, decide which sites you must see and if you have room for a few others! Knowing what you want to do and see in Rome is key to having an enjoyable experience. However, don't forget to find some downtime in between.

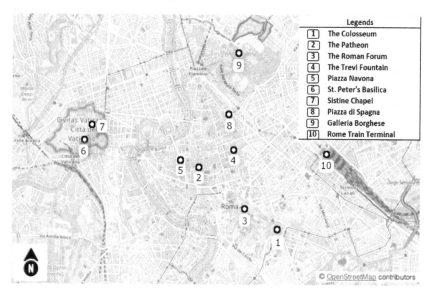

Legends	
1	The Colosseum
2	The Patheon
3	The Roman Forum
4	The Trevi Fountain
5	Piazza Navona
6	St. Peter's Basilica
7	Sistine Chapel
8	Piazza di Spagna
9	Galleria Borghese
10	Rome Train Terminal

© OpenStreetMap contributors

The Colosseum

It would not be a trip to Rome without a trip to the Flavian Amphitheater (most

commonly known as the Colosseum)! The Colosseum is a symbol of greatness in Italy. Standing in the archaeological heart of Rome, it is nearly 2,000 years old—more interesting is that it is still the largest arena in the world today!

Emperor Vespasian of the Flavian Dynasty had the Colosseum commissioned between 70 and 72; it opened in the year 80 by Vespasian's son, Titus, where 100 days of games took place. Since its inauguration, the Colosseum was actively used for over four centuries until the Western Roman Empire ended the gladiator combats in the sixth century. By that time, the arena had some damage due to weather and earthquakes. By the 20th century, about two-thirds of the Colosseum saw further damage due to vandalism, neglect, weather, and other natural disasters. However, despite its challenges, it still stands tall today and hosts several exhibitions and modern shows yearly.

Something to remember when visiting the Colosseum is that security is relatively high to keep everyone safe. If you are traveling with large bags or backpacks, you cannot enter the premises. However, small and medium-sized bags are okay and will be screened by security and walking through a metal detector.

There are tickets you will need to purchase to enter the Colosseum. If you pre-book your tickets, you can skip the line to advance to security. However, be mindful that security checks can take 10 minutes to an hour, depending on the time of day you are going. If you want to avoid being in the bustle of tourists, go earlier in the day, as the Colosseum opens to visitors at 8:30 a.m. (Plus, if you are going to Italy in the summer, you can beat some of the heat by going there in the morning). Here are the ticket prices:

Admission price	Who does it apply to	Additional notes
€ 22	Regular visitors 18 and up	It also includes access to the Roman Forum and Palatine Hill
€ 2	Visitors between 0 and 17 years old.	
€39,90	Guided tour	Colosseum tour with Roman Forum and Palatine Hill
€29,88	Guided tour	Colosseum tour with Roman Forum and Palatine Hill and the arena floor

Roman Forum and Palatine Hill

The Colosseum may overshadow the Roman Forum and Palatine Hill, but it's one place you wouldn't want to miss! (Hence, I included this information in the additional notes to the Colosseum ticket prices.)

Palatine Hill is one of the seven famous hills in Rome and overlooks the Roman

Forum. During ancient Rome, this area was most coveted by aristocrats and emperors. Today, it is an archaeological site where travelers can explore the ruins of Flavian Palace and the Stadium of Domitian.

As for the Roman Forum, historians believe it was in this area where the Roman Republic was founded in 500 B.C.E. by brothers Romulus and Remus. It was the center of ancient Rome, where important political, religious, and social activities occurred, including social gatherings, business affairs, elections, public speeches, and meetings.

While you are wandering around the Roman Forum, check out some of these important buildings:

Temple of Saturn: The Temple of Saturn was the first of its kind, built around 498 B.C.E. It's one of the earliest temples in this region. The name of the building was a dedication to Saturn, the god of agriculture. The Temple of Saturn once served as a treasury (or bank) to manage and keep Rome's money safe.

Senate House: The Senate House, also known as the Curia, was the Roman Senate's council house that was the site for various political events until the seventh century when it was converted to a church.

The Rostra: The Rostra was a stage where people delivered speeches.

The Pantheon

Hours of operation: 9 a.m. to 7 p.m. daily (last entry is at 6 p.m.)

The regular price of admission is €5 (reduced to €3 for visitors between 18 and 25 years old). You can pre-book your tickets online to save waiting in line; however, they can also be purchased in front of the monument.

The Pantheon is one of the oldest and most well-preserved temples in Rome. It was

commissioned in 27 B.C.E. by Marcus Vipsanius Agrippa, who dedicated it to all gods. It was later rebuilt between 112 and 125 by Hadrian, who expanded the temple and reversed its orientation to have a new large square opening at the front of the new temple.

The Pantheon has an impressive dome measuring 142 feet, making it the widest hemispheric dome ever built—it's even bigger than St. Peter's dome! More interesting is that the dome features sunken panels in five rings of 28. The center has an oculus, the only spot allowing natural light in! It's a neat building to experience, especially with its ancient roots.

The Trevi Fountain

The Trevi Fountain (Fontana di Trevi) is one of the most famous fountains in Rome (and the one where everyone goes to make a wish). Not only is it the largest fountain in the city, but it's also one of the finest pieces of work from the Baroque period.

The fountain is almost 100 feet high in front of the Palazzo Poli. The god

underneath the arch is not Neptune (despite what many believe), but Oceanus, the Titan God of the Earth-encircling River Oceanus. You may notice that the seahorses pulling Oceanus reflect two different characteristics: one that looks wild and the other calm—it's believed that these two differentiating features of the seahorses symbolize the varying characteristics between oceans or seas and rivers. To the right of Oceanus is the goddess Heath holding a cup for a snake to drink from. To his left is the goddess Abundance carrying a horn of plenty. Above Heath is the Roman army general Agrippa, known for his work on repairing and renovating the aqueducts to Rome from 45 to 12 B.C.E.

Throwing a coin in the fountain is believed to have started in ancient Rome. Back then, people would turn their back to the fountain, toss the coin in, and drink a cup of water to ensure the thrower would get good fortune and a fast return to Rome. Whether or not you believe in this myth, tossing a couple of coins helps with charities as the coins are collected daily. Also, don't drink the water. While it once supplied water to the people of Rome, it's now recycled water and runs for display only!

Piazza Navona

The Piazza Navona is an important and historical square in Rome as it was built on the remains of the Stadium of Domitian. There are three stunning fountains in

the Piazza Navona. They are the Fontana dei Quattro Fiumi, Fontana del Moro, and Fontana del Nuttuno.

Fontana dei Quattro Fiumi

The Fontana dei Quattro Fiumi is in the center of the Piazza Navona. Four statues on this fountain represent the important rivers where Christianity had spread among the continents. These four rivers include the Nile, the Danube, the Ganges, and Rio de la Plata.

Fontana del Moro

The Fontana del Moro is on the south side of the piazza. It was sculpted in 1575 by Giacomo Della Porta using Pietrasanta marble (holy stone). Its name came from an inspiration of an Ethiopian fighting with a dolphin, but not much else is known about the fountain's history or inspiration. However, it did need to be restored in 1874, and the statues you see on the fountain today are replicas of the original.

Fontana del Nettuno

The Fontana del Nettuno was also sculpted by Della Porta a year before the Fontana del Moro. It remained unfinished for over 300 years until Antonio Della Bitta and Gregorio Zappalà finished it. This fountain symbolizes the Pope's power, who is seen as a world ruler, much like Neptune was a god and ruler of the seas.

You can also stop for lunch or dinner at any restaurant as you admire the area. You may also have the pleasure of being entertained by buskers!

St. Peter's Basilica

It is free to enter St. Peter's Basilica. The hours of operation are as follows:

- From October to March: 7 a.m. to 6:30 p.m.
  - Dome: 8 a.m. to 5:30 p.m.
- From April to September: 7 a.m. to 7 p.m.
  - Dome: 8 a.m. to 6 p.m.

St. Peter's Basilica is the universal seat of the Catholic Church and the Pontifical Chapel and the destination of every pilgrimage in Rome. In addition to being the center of the Roman Catholic Church, it's also the home to several famous works of art celebrating the religion.

The basilica's construction began in 1506 and took 161 years to complete. It earned its name of St. Peter after one of Jesus's twelve disciples of the same name.

The basilica can hold up to 20,000 people. As you walk through it, you will see some impressive works of art, including Bernini's large bronze baldachin called St. Peter's Baldachin. The Pietà by Michelangelo is also in St. Peter's. However, the dome is the most impressive part of the church, designed by Michelangelo, continued by Della Porta, and finally completed by Carlo Maderno in 1614. Gian Lorenzo Bernini added the final additions to the basilica, including St. Peter's Chair and the Baldacchino.

Going to St. Peter's Basilica is an unforgettable experience, and it is worth climbing to the top of the dome, where you can view the square below. If you wish to go to the top, here is what it will cost:

- If you wish to take the elevator to the terrace and climb the remaining 320 steps, it is €8.
- If you wish to forego the elevator and climb all 551 steps to the top, it is €6. Climbing the stairs can feel intimidating as the final part of the ascent is on a narrow and steep spiral staircase. (I promise, it's worth it!)

Sistine Chapel

Hours of operation: The Sistine Chapel is open from Monday to Saturday between 9 a.m. and 6 p.m. (the last chance to buy tickets is before 4 p.m. at the ticket office). It's closed every Sunday except for the last Sunday of each month.

The price to enter the Sistine Chapel is

- €16 for adults
- €8 for children between 6 and 18 years old and students between 19 and 26.
- The admission fees are waived if you visit the chapel on the last Sunday of the month.

Located next to St Peter's, the Sistine Chapel is one of Michelangelo's greatest masterpieces and a treasure of Vatican City, Rome, and the world, as it is the

temple where new popes are chosen and crowned. It was a dedication to the Assumption of the Virgin Mary and was commissioned at the end of the 15th century by Pope Sixtus IV della Rovere.

The Sistine Chapel's construction began in

1473 and was completed in 1481. Its architecture is impressive, but its frescoes that cover the walls and ceilings are something to marvel at as you walk through the chapel. Pope Sixtus IV was looking for artists who could capture the lives of Jesus and Moses in a series of frescoes. He entrusted Michelangelo, Botticelli, Luca Signorelli, and Pietro Perugino with creating this vision on the ceilings and throughout the chapel; Michelangelo was the sole creator of the paintings you see on the ceiling, which took him four years to complete. Of the frescoes, the nine stories from Genesis are the ones that stand out the most; they occupy the central area and include scenes from the *Drunkenness of Noah* and the *Separation of Light from Darkness*.

Guided tours are available if you want to see St. Peter's Basilica and the Sistine Chapel together with a tour of the Vatican Museums. You can reserve these guided tours online, and with them, you can skip the lines and see all three attractions, allowing you to see the essential sights and make good use of your time (especially if it is limited). However, you can also purchase a Rome tourist card to view other attractions, including the Pantheon, Roman Forum, Palatine Hill, and the Colosseum.

Piazza di Spagna and the Spanish Steps

The Piazza di Spagna is one of Rome's famous squares. Its name came from the

Palazzo di Spagna, the Spanish Embassy's seat for the Vatican in this square. This area is in a popular Roman neighborhood with impressive villas dating back to the 17th and 18th centuries on high streets, including the Via dei Condotti, Via Frattina, and Via del Babuino. This area is also popular for shopping at well-known designer shops, including Valentino.

The Spanish Steps in the square (Scalinata di Trinità dei Monti) were built at the start of the 18th century (between 1723 and 1726) to connect the square to the Church of the Holy Trinity of the Mountains (Church of Trinità dei Monti). This staircase is favored among travelers as they love to sit on one of the 135 steps to enjoy the views of the Piazza di Spagna.

Also, in this square, you will see the famous fountain, Fontana della Barcaccia (the Fountain of the Ugly Boat). Bernini designed the fountain, and his son, Gian Lorenzo Bernini, helped him complete it in 1627. While the sculpture has a hilarious name, it's not meant to be ironic. The boat in the fountain refers to a story about the river Tiber flooding in 1598 and stranding an ugly little boat in its wake.

Catacombs of Rome

Beneath the streets just outside of Rome are the catacombs, the former burial grounds dating from the second to fifth centuries used to bury Jewish, pagan, and early Christian Roman citizens. It sounds eerie, but it's a neat piece of Roman history!

The catacombs began as a result of a pagan tradition that involved burning corpses. The Christians disagreed with this tradition, and there was not enough space above ground (so to speak) to bury the dead (plus the cost of land was significant), so the solution was to create underground cemeteries.

The catacombs were created with several subterranean passageways forming labyrinths that run for miles with rows of rectangular niches. When someone died, they would be wrapped in a sheet and placed in a niche, and covered with gravestones made from marble or baked clay. As you see in cemeteries today, the names of the deceased were also carved into the gravestone along with a Christian symbol.

Rome has more than 60 catacombs, but only five of them are open for your exploring (if you dare):

Catacombs of San Sebastiano: This catacomb is 7.4 miles long and is open between 9 a.m. and 12 p.m. and 2 p.m. and 5 p.m., Monday to Saturday.
Catacombs of Callisto: This catacomb is 12.4 miles long and is open between 9 a.m. and 12 p.m. and 2 p.m. and 5 p.m. between Tuesday and Thursday.
Catacombs of Domitilla: This catacomb is more than 9.3 miles long and is open from Monday to Wednesday from 9 a.m. to 12 p.m. and 2 p.m. to 5 p.m.
Catacombs of Sant'Agnese: This catacomb is open between 9 a.m. and 12 p.m. and 4 p.m. and 6 p.m. daily except for Sunday mornings and Monday afternoons.
Catacombs of Priscilla: This catacomb is open between Tuesday and Sunday from 9 a.m. to 12 p.m. and 2 p.m. to 5 p.m.

The best way to explore the catacombs is by reserving a tour (given the short opening times). Otherwise, here is the pricing: adults €8 and children 15 and under €5

Galleria Borghese and Villa Borghese

Immerse yourself in one of the largest private art collections in the world at the Galleria Borghese! Within the 20 rooms are antiques, sculptures, paintings, and many notable works from the Renaissance, including masterpieces created by Raphael, Caravaggio, Titian, Bernini, Canova, and Corregio.

The Villa Borghese on Pincio Hill is just a short distance from the gallery. The park is 80 hectares and has various beautiful sights, including.

- Villa Giulia, Pope Julius III's 16th-century summer residence. This is now a museum displaying Etruscan art.
- Villa Medici, a 16th-century mansion that is now the French Academy in Rome; guided tours are available if you're interested in checking it out.
- Bioparco, a 100-year-old zoo. At its inauguration, it was ahead of its time and had plenty of greenery for the animals to roam instead of keeping them in small enclosures with bars.
- several pavilions from the 1911 World's Fair along the Viale delle Belle Arti. You'll also find the national museum for modern and contemporary art, Galleria Nazionale d'Arte Moderna, mainly displaying paintings and sculptures by Italian artists throughout 75 rooms.
- Tempio di Esculapio, a temple from the 18th century dedicated to the gods of medicines. It's near the park's lake where you can rent a rowboat.

	Hours of operation	Admission fees
Galleria Borghese	Tuesday to Sunday from 9 a.m. to 7 p.m. (the last admission is at 5 p.m.)	Adults: From €25
	On Thursdays, the gallery is open until 9 p.m.	Children aged 6 to 17: €6
	Groups will enter every two hours.	You should book your tickets in advance as they only allow 360 people in the gallery per two-hour tour.
Villa Borghese	The park is open from sunrise to sunset.	As this is a public park and garden, it is free to visit and roam around to your little heart's content!

Things to Experience and Enjoy in Rome

While there are several places you should check out in Rome, don't forget about the experiences that can encompass your time in the Eternal City!

Wander Around Trastevere

Trastevere is a lovely neighborhood in Rome with a bohemian and peaceful atmosphere capturing the hearts of travelers. This neighborhood was once a

working-class neighborhood on the opposite side of the Tiber River. Due to its proximity to the river, it was home to many fishermen and sailors. When the Roman imperial period came around (between 27 B.C.E. and 14 A.D.), this district became immensely wealthy, and influential figures, like Julius Caesar, chose to build their villas in the neighborhood.

You will learn that tourists love wandering through Trastevere as it has several narrow alleyways, cobblestoned streets, and houses from the medieval period to see. However, there are several unique shops and medieval churches worth exploring too. Some of these medieval churches include Piazzi di Santa Maria, Basilica Santa Maria, and Basilica of Santa Cecilia.

In addition to looking at the various sites in the nooks and crannies of this neighborhood, it's also fun to be in during the evening! It becomes livelier in the various restaurants, pizzerias, and trattorias to check out and mingle with fellow travelers.

Something fun to do: If you are in Rome on a Sunday, go to Trastevere in the morning as a flea market is held until 2 p.m., selling various items from clothing to antiques.

Taste Authentic Roman Cuisine and Local Specialties

Everywhere you go in Italy, you will find different traditions and cuisine styles, making eating in Italy more fun for your tastebuds! Many don't realize that much of the Roman cuisine today stems from traditions based on poverty and what ingredients were available. That may seem limited, but you'd be surprised by the endless possibilities of meals for you to enjoy while in Rome. It may seem easy to stick to the basics, but trying some of their authentic dishes is a must, especially since Rome has particular types of pasta that you won't find anywhere else in Italy, such as pasta alla carbonara, carciofi alla Romana, amatriciana, and pasta cacio e pepe.

But before I get ahead of myself and list all of the pasta, here are some other delicious delicacies:

Coda alla vaccinara: This is a classic Italian dish originating from Rome, featuring oxtail slow-cooked in a rich tomato sauce with celery, carrots, onions, and red wine. The tender, flavorful meat falls off the bone, creating a hearty and comforting stew.

Pomodori con riso: This baked dish is a popular Italian dish made by stuffing ripe tomatoes with a mixture of rice, herbs, and sometimes meat or cheese. The tomatoes are then baked until tender, resulting in a delightful combination of flavors and textures that celebrate the essence of Italian cuisine.

Filetti di baccala: An appetizer made with deep-fried salted cod filets. The preparation involves soaking dried cod to remove its saltiness and then frying the tender fillets until crispy and golden. Served with lemon wedges, this delicacy offers a delightful contrast of textures and flavors.

Gnocchi alla Romana: This is a delightful Italian dish hailing from Rome. Unlike traditional potato gnocchi, it's made with semolina flour, milk, butter, and cheese. The dough is rolled, cut into discs, layered with butter and cheese, then baked until golden. The result is a creamy, comforting, and indulgent delicacy.

Ciambelle al vino: These are Italian wine cookies, often enjoyed during special occasions. Made with red or white wine, flour, sugar, and a touch of olive oil, they have a crisp exterior and a tender interior. These delightful treats are often flavored with lemon or anise, offering a delightful taste of Italy's culinary traditions.

Maritozzi: Maritozzi is a delectable Italian sweet bun originating from Rome. These soft, fluffy rolls are enriched with eggs, butter, and sugar and then filled with whipped cream, raisins, and candied orange peel. Often enjoyed for breakfast or as a snack, Maritozzi offers a delightful taste of Roman pastry craftsmanship.

Crostata di ricotta: Crostata di Ricotta is a luscious Italian dessert featuring a

buttery shortcrust pastry filled with a creamy mixture of ricotta cheese, sugar, eggs, and citrus zest. Baked until golden, the crostata is then dusted with powdered sugar, resulting in a delightful balance of flavors and a dessert beloved across Italy.

Visit the Baths of Caracalla

Hours of operation: Tuesday to Sunday from 9 a.m. to 6:30 p.m. and Mondays from 9 a.m. to 2 p.m.

Admission fee: €13

The Baths of Caracalla are a great example of what Imperial baths looked like in Rome. These baths were built between 212 and 216 under the recommendation of Marcus Aurelius Augustus. They were specifically commissioned to be a spa, but they also became a place for Romans to spend their time leisurely, play sports, take a stroll, and study. In other words, aside from it being a spa, it was a space for Romans to mingle with one another in addition to relaxing.

The Baths of Caracalla had three rooms with different temperatures to suit the guests' needs, two gyms, and a sauna. The hottest bath was in the caldarium, a circular room with seven pools. These pools were heated by fires below to reach temperatures of 100.4°F.

The next room was the tepidarium, which had two pools with warm water, making it the most relaxing set of pools in the entire complex. It was also decorated with marble and mosaics.

The last room was called the frigidarium, located in the center and connected to the other rooms. As you can guess by the name, it had four cold pools and a decorative fountain that once was nearly entirely covered in marble.

In addition to the three rooms with differing bath temperatures, the complex had an Olympic-sized swimming pool topped with bronze mirrors to use as heaters.

There were two of the libraries, but only one survives today. The libraries had books in Greek and Latin.

See an Opera at the Teatro dell'Opera di Roma

The Teatro dell'Opera di Roma, also known as Teatro Costanzi, was built on the former site of the Eliogabalo. It earned its name based on the founding entrepreneur Domenico Costanzi, who wanted a theater to host opera and ballet performances.

Achille Sfondrini was entrusted with creating this theater as he had specialization in restoring and building theaters. The Teatro dell'Opera di Roma was designed in a neo-Renaissance style to use for an acoustic performance. The theater was officially inaugurated on November 27, 1880, with Rossini's opening performance of *Semiramide*. Since its establishment, this theater has seen many prestigious operas pass through its stage. You can catch an opera performance in the building during winter. However, performances will move outside to the Baths of Caracalla during the warmer months to offer a different experience.

Shop Along Via del Corso

Bordered by the Piazza Venezia and Piazza del Popolo, the Via del Corso is nearly a mile long with several shops to match all budget and shopping needs. When the road was built (between 270 and 275 A.D.), it wasn't meant to be a shopping promenade but a wall to help defend Rome from the Germanic tribes invading the Empire.

Since it was built, it has seen several fascinating historical periods.

- During the Imperial Age, emperors Augustus and Nero were buried here due to the low population in the area.
- During the Middle Ages, Via del Corso was practically a ghost town, primarily due to Tiber flooding.

- In the mid-15th century, Via del Corso acquired a new life thanks to Pope Paul II. He loved spectacles and decided to have a beautiful palace built in Piazza Venezia as a place of residence for himself. Around this time, the Via del Corso also became the Carnival festival's world capital, with the celebrations beginning on February 9, 1466. Due to its length, it was a great street to host competitions.
- After July 30, 1900, when King Umberto I of Savoy was assassinated, Via del Corso was renamed Corso Umberto; in 1944, its name changed again to Corso del Popolo. Two years later, it went back to being the Via del Corso.

As you walk along the Via del Corso (with this little history lesson in mind), be sure to take in some of the architectural sites as they represent some timeless art nouveau styles. There are also several noble residences along this route, such as the Palazzo Bonaparte, the home of Napoleon's mother. You'll also see several churches, including the Basilica of SS. Ambrose and Charles. Lastly, if you love literature, the House Museum of Johann Wolfgang von Goethe is worth checking out!

Walk Along the Tiber River

The Tiber River is the longest in Italy—about 252 miles long—and has been an identifying mark of Rome since the Great Empire. However, it's also a river with an interesting legend involving Remus and Romulus. Legend has it that when these two were newborns, they were to be drowned in the Tiber River.

Legends aside, historians are confident Rome was established around 753 B.C.E. along these banks. At the time, the river was a border between the Etruscans on the west, the Sabines on the east, and the Latins who lived south of the river.

The Tiber River was prominent in building the Roman economy as several merchant ships moved through its waters. As we discussed earlier in this chapter, Trastevere was the neighborhood that housed many sailors and fishermen due to its proximity to the water, allowing these men to provide for the city.

As you stroll along the river, you will notice 26 bridges connecting the banks. There are several new ones; however, many old ones have survived the centuries. One of the pedestrian bridges, Pone Sisto, is one worth walking over. This stone bridge dates back to the Medieval Ages and was dedicated to Pope Sixtus IV. You may also notice that the Tiber River flows close to some famous Roman spots, such as Testaccio and the Trastevere neighborhoods.

There is one island on this river called Tiber Island. It houses the Fatebenefratelli Hospital, established in 1585 by Pope Gregory XIII. You can access this island by the Ponte Cestio and the Pone Fabricio bridges, each built in 46 and 52 B.C.E., respectively.

Staying in Rome

Since Rome is a big city to visit, figuring out where you want to stay may feel overwhelming. As always, choosing an area that is relatively close to public transportation is a good start, but keep in mind what you would like to do and see while in Rome!

Near the Pantheon, Piazza Navona, and Campo de Fiori

The Pantheon, Piazza Navona, and Campo de Fiori are right in the heart of Rome and close to several landmarks. In this area, you can immerse yourself in a Baroque atmosphere in Piazza Navona, the Campo de Fiori's market filled with busy energy, and the Pantheon temple that's been a staple of Rome for over 2,000 years. The significant part about staying here is that it makes it accessible to walk to other major attractions, including the Colosseum, Trevi Fountain, and St. Peter's Square, which means you don't necessarily require public transportation. Here are some hotel options to consider:

Little Queen Pantheon: As a budget-friendly hotel, the Little Queen Pantheon is a stone's throw away from the Trevi Fountain, with stunning city views. It's also close to several other points of interest, including the Spanish Steps.
Boutique Hotel Campo de' Fiori: If you're looking for a bit of an upper-scale hotel, the Boutique Hotel Campo de' Fiori is close to the market and has several restaurants. It also features a terrace with a full panoramic view of Rome!

Near the Piazza di Spagna and Spanish Steps

The Piazza di Spagna and Spanish Steps area is excellent if you're looking to move from place to place on foot. However, this area also has two metro stops if you want to move further than the central Rome area. Here are some of the places that are recommended for the Piazza di Spagna and Spanish steps area to check out:

Hassler Roma: If you love to mingle among celebrities, the Hassler Roma is the hotel many love staying in when they come to Rome! This hotel is at the top of the Spanish Steps and offers gorgeous rooms, free wellness facilities, and panoramic views of Rome. In addition to being near metro stations, the Hassler Roma Hotel offers free shuttle services to take you to shops in the surrounding area.
Palazzo Nainer: The Palazzo Nainer is on an exclusive street leading to the Piazza del Popolo and Spanish steps. This hotel is in a 19th-century building, surrounded by antique shops (if you love going antiquing), art galleries, and designer shops. When you are done exploring for the day, head up to their rooftop garden, where you can enjoy the views of Rome's historic center!

Near Trastevere

Since Trastevere has a peaceful and bohemian vibe, staying here is a lovely option if you're looking to step away from the busyness of the city and immerse yourself in a different kind of energy when you have seen everything you wanted to see. Here are some excellent hotel options to look into in Trastevere:

Hotel Santa Maria: Set in a 16th-century former convent, this peaceful hotel offers a stay unlike anything else with personalized service to meet your needs. All guest rooms look into an internal garden with orange trees, flowers, and other Mediterranean greenery.
B&B Suites Trastevere: This is an excellent hotel for a home-like feel. Many guests who have stayed here have raved about the owner, who takes excellent care of her guests and serves delicious breakfast and snacks throughout the day. As for location, this hotel is near public transportation to get you to all of the major attractions.

Near the Vatican

If you want to stay near Vatican City, you will want to stay in the Prati district, which is adjacent to it, especially if you intend to spend most of your time exploring St. Peter's Basilica and surrounding museums. What is neat about this area is that Vatican City is somewhat of a small city of its own within Rome, giving a different way to experience Rome altogether! Here's where to stay:

Domus Terenzio: The Domus Terenzio is 10 minutes from St. Peter's Square. It has a lovely terrace to relax in as well as modern rooms.
Starhotels Michelangelo Rome: This hotel is steps from St. Peter's Square and is within walking distance of the Sistine Chapel and Vatican Museums.

What NOT to Do in Rome

Rome is filled with a lot of rich cultural history, and it's also one of the most iconic cities in the world. With so many monuments taking you back to Ancient Rome, delicious cuisine, and several other pieces that make Rome the city everyone knows, it's a fantastic place to explore and physically be. However, while visiting Rome is thrilling in its unique ways, it's also important to remember several things you shouldn't do (including carving your name on the Colosseum). This section will look into some of the important pitfalls you should avoid while in Rome.

Don't Forget to Book Your Reservation
As Rome is a popular city to visit in Italy, it should be no surprise that you should reserve your tickets to several attractions in advance. Be sure to book your tickets online ahead of when you plan to go to the major attractions to avoid the headache of not being able to get in.

Don't Forget to Check the Opening Days and Times
While I have provided you with several hours of operation, there is always the possibility that some attractions may be closed on specific days, so it's a good idea to double-check. On the upside, when you book your tickets in advance, the website

for the attractions will also indicate if visiting the site that day you want to go is possible.

Don't Eat in the Main Piazzas
A ban prevents you from eating near the famous fountains throughout Rome. It may seem like a silly rule, but it's in place to help preserve the monuments and keep them clean.

Do not underestimate the distance between attractions

Rome's landmarks and attractions are spread out across the city. Avoid assuming that you can easily walk to each destination. Plan your itinerary accordingly and consider using public transportation or taxis when necessary. Use apps like 'Google Maps' to check walking time from one place to another.

Do not dine in tourist trap restaurants

Be cautious of restaurants located near popular tourist attractions that are specifically designed to attract tourists. These establishments often charge high prices for mediocre food. Seek recommendations from locals or do some research to find authentic and quality dining experiences.

Don't Jump into the Fountains

The film La Dolce Vita featured scenes of the actors jumping into the Trevi Fountain, but that is a big no-no! Rome can get very hot in the summer, but don't jump or put your feet into the fountains or wells, as it can land you with a fine.

Rome has a captivating history that many of us think we know until we realize there is more to the Eternal City than meets the eye. We all have marveled at the Colosseum, but seeing it up close is a different feeling altogether as you imagine what life was like within its walls all those centuries ago. You may feel similar feelings about this if you visit other iconic landmarks like St Peter's Square.

As you spend time in Rome, remember that exploring is only half the fun! Remember to immerse yourself in some activities and experiences, like wandering around the Tiber River and eating some traditional Roman cuisine you won't get anywhere else.

Rome is a splendid city and one of its kind, much like all other cities throughout Italy. But there is still more to see and explore in this boot-shaped country. Let's move on to Naples, an area that has ties to ancient Greece and is described as majestic.

Chapter 8

Naples—Dos and Don'ts

N aples, or Napoli in Italian, is a popular destination for tourists traveling further into the Mediterranean region. The history of this region goes back to the ancient Greek era, which founded Naples in the eighth century B.C.E. The name Napoli came from the Greek word Neapolis, which translates to "new town" or "new city."

As Naples is a part of the Greek heritage, this city did not join Italy's country officially until October 1860, when Italy's unification movement took place. With its joining to Italy, Naples became the third largest city in the country (next to Milan and Rome).

Naples is also the city where our favorite food, pizza, was created. The first pizzeria, Antica Pizzeria Port'Alba, opened in Naples before the unification in 1830, and it's still open today and serving all types of slices. Naples is also where the classic Margherita pizza was made—it earned its name after Queen Margherita Teresa Giovanni visited Naples during the 19th century.

With so much to explore, you never know what you will find when you wander the winding streets of Naples!

What to DO in Naples

To the average person, Naples can feel like the most overwhelming city to visit in Italy, mainly because of its size. But it's a stunning area to go to with beautiful waterfront views, mountains in the distance, and a city full of artistic wonder, making it a one-of-a-kind experience for each traveler who walks the streets.

As Naples is a large city, you should know off-hand that it is divided into various sections and neighborhoods. They are all reachable by foot or public transportation, so you don't need to worry about having a car or taking a taxi everywhere! With that in mind, what *do* you do in such a large city?

Legends
1. San Carlo Theatre
2. Naples Cathedral
3. Piazza del Plebiscito
4. Castle Nuovo
5. National Archeological Museum
6. Castle dell'Ovo
7. Cappella Sansevero

© OpenStreetMap contributors

San Carlo Theater

Hours of operation: By guided tour only from Monday to Saturday at 10:30 a.m., 11:30 a.m., 12:30 p.m., 2:30 p.m., 3:30 p.m., and 4:30 p.m.

Admission fees: The costs of the guided tours are as follows: 1) €9 for adults (30 and up) 2) €7 for young adults under 30 and seniors over 60 and 3) €4 for children under 10

One of the first stops you should take while in Naples is visiting the San Carlo Theater (Teatro di San Carlo). The theater was built in a stunning neoclassical building in 1737 when King Charles III of Naples wanted a bigger royal theater. It was embellished with gorgeous blue and gold decorations and exquisite architecture during its construction. Sadly, in 1816, the theater suffered damage from a significant fire. It was restored with the auditorium rebuilt to be a horseshoe, painted with frescoes, and updated to have red and gold decor instead of the former blue and gold. Unfortunately, that would not be the first time this theater experienced damage as it was bombed during the Second World War.

Considering the damage it suffered, it remains a lavish venue for opera and ballet performances and is one of the oldest-running opera houses in the world. You can take guided tours of the main auditorium, the two foyers, and the royal box. However, if you're interested in experiencing an opera or ballet performance, you may want to check out their schedule to see what is available. Tickets run from €20.

Naples Cathedral

Hours of Operation: 8 a.m. to 12:30 p.m. and 4:30 p.m. to 7 p.m.

Admission is free unless you plan to go to the baptistery, which will cost €2.

One of the next places you should explore in Naples is the Naples Cathedral, also known as the Cathedral of Assumption of Mary or the Duomo. Whichever name you go by, this is the main cathedral in Naples, and it was built between 1299 and 1314 at the request of Carlo III D'Angiò, the King of Naples.

At a glance, you will see that this cathedral is a fusion of Gothic, Baroque, and neo-Gothic styles to reflect its long history. Inside, it is beautifully detailed with bronze railing, grand altars, and detailed frescoes that display some of Naples' earlier Christian art.

Piazza del Plebiscito

The Piazza del Plebiscito is a gigantic, elegant square in the center of Naples,

surrounded by statues and four important historical and artistic buildings: the Royal Palace, the Prefecture, the Salerno Palace, and the San Francesco di Paola Basilica. The Royal Palace was the first building commissioned by Don Pedro de Toledo, a Spanish nobleman. Once the Royal Palace was completed, Domenico Fontana, a Renaissance architect, designed and added the rest of the square and surrounding buildings. The Piazza del Plebiscito is a great space to escape the busyness of Naples and easily access other points of interest in the area.

Castel Nuovo

Hours of operation: Monday to Saturday between 9 a.m. and 7 p.m.

Admission fees: €6 for adults and free for visitors under 18.

A trip to a castle in any foreign country is always fun—especially in the heart of a city! Castel Nuovo (translated as "New Castle" in English) was initially commissioned in the 13th century by King Charles I of Anjou. However, it's more than just a castle or a royal seat. It served as a place to host several writers and artists, including Boccaccio, Giotto, and Petrarch.

More interesting is that the fortress you'll visit on your trip is not the original one commissioned, but a rebuild of it. The rebuild occurred in the 15th century when the Spanish Empire took over Naples, and Alfonso V of Aragon created a new castle following the Medieval Renaissance style.

As you wander through the castle, be sure to take in the view from the towering walls as they give you an excellent view of the bay. Additionally, you can check out a collection of art from the 17th to early 20th centuries inside the castle.

National Archeological Museum of Naples

Hours of operation: Wednesday to Monday from 9 a.m. to 7:30 p.m. (closed on Tuesdays)

Admission fees: €15 (reduced price is €2)

The National Archeological Museum of Naples contains an extensive collection of items from the Roman art heritage, with much of the collection connected to Charles III of Bourbon.

This museum is a must for all tourists as it allows you to journey through ancient Roman times and Naples's roots. You will see all sorts of relics, including mosaics representing the Battle of Issues, a famous depiction of Alexander the Great, and a Secret Cabinet that unveils a world of Herculaneum and Pompeii Herculaneum brothel.

Castel dell'Ovo

Hours of operation: Monday to Saturday from 9 a.m. to 7:30 p.m. (with the last entry at 7 p.m.) and Sundays from 9 a.m. to 2 p.m. (with the last entry at 1:30 p.m.)

Castel dell'Ovo (the "Egg Castle") is the oldest castle in Naples along the seafront on an ancient island called the Isolotto di Megaride. The castle was built in the first century B.C.E. by Lucius Licinius. After an increase in church power and the Roman Empire ended, the castle was transformed into a monastery, which remained in place for the next five centuries. Over those years, the castle suffered damage from various wars. However, by 1975, Castel dell'Ovo was restored to being a castle.

For another small tidbit about the castle, its name has an interesting legend attached to it. According to legend, the Castel dell'Ovo earned its name when poet Virgil hid an egg in the dungeon. It's believed that if the egg were to be broken, the castle and Naples would be destroyed.

Castel dell'Ovo is accessible by foot, and admission is free.

Cappella Sansevero

Hours of operation: 9 a.m. to 7 p.m. daily (except Tuesdays when it is closed). The last entry into the museum is at 6:30 p.m.

Cappella Sansevero is a popular chapel and art museum for tourists, as it is the home of the famous Veiled Christ sculpture, created in the 18th century. The sculpture is so realistic it will give you chills. However, the rest of the art throughout the museum is equally impressive, including several other allegorical statues watching over the Veiled Christ.

Cappella Sansevero also has a quirky exhibition called the Anatomical Machines. Within the glass cases, you will see skeletons of a man and woman displaying a visible circulatory system.

There is a visitor limit to Cappella Sansevero, and booking your tickets in advance is recommended. Tickets are €8 for adults, €5 for visitors between 10 and 25 years old, and free for kids nine and under. If you book online, there is a booking fee of €2.

Things to Experience and Enjoy in Naples

There are so many things to explore and discover within the city limits of Naples, especially since the city has a rich history! However, trips aren't always meant to be about seeing all the sites—they should also include experiences and adventures! This section will look into different experiences you can add to your Italian adventure to have exciting stories to share with your friends and family when you go home.

Visit Mount Vesuvius

Hours of operation: 9 a.m. to 6 p.m. daily

In the southeast distance of Naples is a large mountain called Mount Vesuvius—if you're an adventurer, this experience is for you! (And seriously, who doesn't love marveling at mountains and volcanoes? They're so cool!)

According to the locals, Vesuvius protects Naples, which sounds ironic given the fact that it is an active volcano and one of the most studied ones due to its eruptive history and the fact that it is a composite volcano (which means it will erupt again, though it's not known when). Either way, people who love hiking enjoy going to the Vesuvius National Park, where they can hike the mountain to see the volcanic landscape and walk around the crater.

Touring Mount Vesuvius has several guided tour options, so you should check out their national park website for more information and to see what is available. Otherwise, tickets start from €20,30.

Walk Along Spaccanapoli

The Spaccanapoli (the Naples splitter) is one of the three main roads that went through ancient Neapolis when it was established in 580 B.C.E., splitting the city into two (north side and south side). It may not seem like much to the naked eye yet, but as you wander through the narrow street, you'll see people talking from their balconies, Vespas transporting people to various destinations, and workers hammering hammers in artisan workshops, making it the vibrant heart of Naples.

Begin your walk at the Piazza del Gesù, and soon enough, you will find yourself in the bustling heart of Naples. Your stroll will take you past several piazzas, churches, palaces along the way, and restaurants, bakeries, and gift shops. Walking the Spaccanapoli will give you an authentic taste of Neapolitan life.

Santa Chiara Religious Complex's Colorful Cloisters

Hours of operation: Monday to Saturday between 9:30 a.m. and 5:30 p.m. and Sundays from 10 a.m. to 2:30 p.m.

The Complex of Santa Chiara in Naples is one of the most appreciated monuments in the city. While this building has a beautiful monastery, basilica, a small museum, and a religious library, it's most famous for its colorful and detailed cloisters throughout.

The Santa Chiara Religious Complex was commissioned by King Robert d'Angiò and was built between 1313 and 1340. Many features date back to the 14th century, but the cloisters throughout the complex were designed during the 17th century. Every image is so colorful, eye-catching, and stunning as it captures the rural life of scenes of the Mediterranean seaside. In addition, prepare to be amazed by the Rococo-style Majorca tiles and frescoes on the porticoes around the courtyard. It is free to enter the church. However, if you want to wander around the cloisters, it is €6.

The Catacombs of Naples

The Catacombs of Naples is another enter-if-you-dare experience, and much like the catacombs in Rome, these catacombs serve as another critical piece of Italian history. These catacombs are believed to have originally housed San Gennaro, a protector saint whose body was laid to rest in the fifth century. From there on, the catacombs were the destination for pilgrimages until the ninth century. After that, they were forgotten about until their rediscovery in the 1600s.

There are two levels in these catacombs—the lower one, of course, being the oldest, going back to the second century. You'll learn more about the types of tombs and how they correspond to particular social classes. It's not as creepy as it may seem (and I was kidding about it being an enter-if-you-dare attraction). It is neat to see how these catacombs have been created and maintained throughout the centuries, in addition to some of the frescoes. To visit the catacombs, you will need to join a guided tour.

Peek Inside the Royal Palace

Hours of operation: Thursday to Tuesday from 9 a.m. to 8 p.m. The Royal Palace is closed on Wednesdays.

If you are in the Piazza del Plebiscito, it's worth going into the Royal Palace. This palace dates back to the 1600s and was designed by Domenico Fontaine. From the 1600s until 1946, the Royal Palace served as a monarchical power seat in Naples. It saw many power shifts in its years, first with the Spanish, then the Austrians, then the Bourbons, and finally by the House of Savoy.

When you enter the Royal Palace, you'll start in the apartment where you will see the Royal Chapel, the Court Theater, the Hall of Hercules, the Apartment of

Etiquette, and the Staircase of Honor. In these rooms are several tapestries, marble sculptures, paintings, and frescoes depicting a rich history. Outside, you can wander through the courtyard and romantic garden to see unique features, including the Hanging Garden that overlooks the Gulf of Naples and Mount Vesuvius. To see the Royal Palace, it is 1) €10 for adults 2) €2 for visitors between 18 and 24 years old, and 3) free for visitors under 18

Indulge in Neapolitan Pastries

We're back to the delicious food-tasting portion—because it's Italy, after all! There are many delicacies to enjoy throughout Italy. However, I loved the pastries in Naples, where you can eat traditional and modern desserts. These sweets are some of the most famous in the world! A couple of the pastries you should try include

Babà: Baba, an Italian dessert with Neapolitan origins, is a yeasted cake soaked in a syrup made with rum or other liqueurs. The cake is light and spongy, absorbing the sweet syrup, resulting in a moist and flavorful treat. Often served with whipped cream or fruit, Baba is a delightful indulgence.

Sfogliatella: Sfogliatella is a classic Italian pastry hailing from Naples. Its flaky, layered dough encases a filling of ricotta cheese, semolina, candied fruit, and orange zest. The "sfogliatella riccia" has a shell-like appearance, while "sfogliatella frolla" has a smoother shell.

Ricotta e pera: Ricotta e Pera is a simple yet delightful Italian dessert. Ripe pears are poached in sugar and vanilla and then served with a generous dollop of creamy ricotta cheese. The contrast between the sweet, tender pears and the smooth, slightly tangy ricotta creates a perfect harmony of flavors.

Torta Caprese: Torta Caprese, an iconic Italian dessert from Capri, is a gluten-free chocolate almond cake. Made with ground almonds, cocoa, sugar, butter, and eggs, it has a rich, dense texture and an intense chocolate flavor. Often dusted with powdered sugar, this decadent treat celebrates the unique taste of Southern Italy.

Eat Neapolitan Pizza at a Local Pizzeria

There's pizza, and then there is Neapolitan pizza (pizza Napoletana). Neapolitan pizza is a type of pizza that comes from Naples. The pizza is made with fresh ingredients, including basil, raw tomatoes, fresh mozzarella, and olive oil, all on a basic dough. I am sorry to report that fancy toppings are not allowed (sorry, pineapple pizza lovers)! Neapolitan pizza is much saucier than traditional pizza, so you can't expect to pick up a slice. Instead, these pizzas are baked to be about 10 to 12 inches in diameter. These mouth-watering and delicious pizzas make for a perfect light lunch or snack!

Take a Boat Tour Along the Bay of Naples

There is much to see, do, and experience within Naples, but have you ever imagined what it might look like from afar? A boat tour along the Bay of Naples gives you a different view of the region. It's a fantastic way to see the skyline of the city and Mount Vesuvius. Several boat tours are available, and some will take you to the Island of Capri and the Amalfi Coast.

Staying in Naples

Where to stay in the third biggest Italian city? That is the question! Depending on how long you intend to be in Naples, your budget, and why you are going there, one of these districts may serve you better than others.

Chiaia

Of the various districts in Naples, Chiaia is one of the safest spots to stay in. It's in the southern part of Naples in the Spanish Quarter and is excellent for those looking for a romantic getaway. Most hotels are set in historic buildings, with several independent boutiques and antique shops along the streets. This area is especially amazing, with incredible views of Naples's Bay, Mount Vesuvius, and Capri. Some hotels to check out include

Micalò Art Rooms: A hotel for those on a budget, the Micalò Art Rooms is set near the Mappatella Beach and has a shared lounge! Some rooms have balconies that allow you to see the city (which is an excellent way to start your day).

The Britannique Hotel Naples: The Britannique Hotel Naples is a 10-minute walk from the shopping district. Depending on the room you get, you may have a view of the Gulf of Naples.

Lungomare Caracciolo

Lungomare Caracciolo is a great place to stay if you're traveling with your family. This area has a beautiful seafront that extends down Naples's coastline, which you can reach by foot or public transportation. This area is lovely to walk around, has several restaurants and cafés, and if you're here on New Year's Eve, you'll be lucky to watch a fireworks show! Here are some places to consider staying:

Palazzo Chiatamone: The Palazzo Chiatamone is another budget-friendly hotel that's relatively close to Mappatella Beach. It's also not overly far from the Castel Nuovo and the Piazza del Plebiscito.

Grand Hotel Santa Lucia: Located near the heart of Naples, the Grand Hotel Santa Lucia offers modern and luxurious rooms and is right on the harbor front of Naples. This hotel is set in a building from the 20th century and is styled in an Art-Nouveau design!

Port of Naples

The Port of Naples is the largest in the country and Mediterranean. Here, you will see several yachts, superyachts, sailboats, cargo ships, and cruise ships docking in the port. It's also near several of the major attractions in Naples, which supports why it's a bustling district! This area can be more expensive given its location, but if you're only going to be here for a day or two, the Port of Naples is a convenient option. Here are a couple of hotels to check out:

Eurostars Hotel Excelsior: The Eurostars Hotel Excelsior overlooks the Bay of Naples, best viewed from their rooftop restaurant and terrace! If you're looking to visit nearby attractions, such as the Piazza del Plebiscito or the Royal Palace, it's about a 10-minute walk!

Smart Hotel Napoli: Don't be fooled! This hotel is budget-friendly and four-star, with a shared lounge and bar. It's also near several points of interest, including the Royal Palace.

What NOT to Do in Naples

We are at the point in this chapter that discusses what you shouldn't do when you're in Naples. There isn't a whole lot (aside from the obvious things we have discussed in previous chapters, so we'll keep it short and to the point.

Don't Go to Scampia and Secondigliano
If you have never visited Naples before, some people may say it's an unsafe region to go to. However, nearly every country has areas that could be safer. That said, Scampia and Secondigliano are two neighborhoods that you should not venture to in Naples—they are two of the most dangerous. There are also no tourist attractions, so there's no reason to go.

Do not rely on public transportation without caution
While public transportation can be a convenient way to get around Naples, be aware of pickpockets, especially on crowded buses or trains. Keep your belongings secure and be cautious of your surroundings.

Do not judge the city based on initial impressions
Naples is a vibrant and energetic city, but it may appear chaotic or run-down in some areas. Give it a chance and explore beyond first impressions. You'll discover its hidden gems, rich history, and the warm hospitality of the locals.

Do not rely on unofficial tour guides
Be cautious of individuals offering unsolicited tour guide services or claiming to have exclusive access to attractions. Stick to licensed tour operators and official guides to ensure accurate information and a safe experience.

Don't Wait in Long Lines
Instead of waiting in long lines to get into attractions, let yourself get lost in the city and historic center to feel the energy Naples offers. Allow your inner adventurer to follow the city so you can admire old shops and watch how Neapolitans connect. (Also, remember, in this day and age, you can prebook tickets ahead of time to save you the headache and hassle!)

Naples is a stunning region in Italy with so much rich history, stemming way before it became a part of the country! There are many things to do, discover, and experience in Naples, especially pizza! As you spend time in Naples, be sure to check out some of the major attractions within the city, but also allow your adventure to take you to places like Mount Vesuvius and along the Gulf of Naples.

Although Naples has an exciting and different piece of history compared to other parts of Italy, we also can't forget about Pompeii, which also has some fascinating pieces encompassing the country and how we have come to know and understand it today.

Chapter 9

Pompeii—Dos and Don'ts

S tanding tall in the distance of Pompeii (*Pompei*), the people in this region were going about their days—little did they know that a volcano was brewing its lava to shoot into the sky and cause massive destruction in the year 79.

That volcano is Mount Vesuvius; it's the one you were introduced to in the last chapter. When it erupted in 79, it had remained quiet and uneventful for 1,800 years—so yes, naturally, no one knew that it was a volcano! Since its eruption in 79, it's been active! It erupted six times during the 18th century, eight times in the 19th century, and three times in the 20th, with the last eruption happening on March 17, 1944. In that wake of destruction, the volcano rained down basketball-sized lava rocks, covered the surrounding areas with a meter of ash, and slowly moved the scathing hot volcanic rock, burning everything in its path. It sounds dramatic, but volcanos do tend to make an entrance.

The volcano aside, what is so neat about Pompeii? Pompeii is one of the most significant archaeological sites in the world, providing evidence of Roman civilization before Mount Vesuvius erupted. When Mount Vesuvius erupted, you can only imagine how tragic its impact was. Pompeii was once a lively area that swiftly came to a standstill. After the eruption, Pompeii remained undiscovered for centuries, its dark history hidden. However, since its rediscovery, it has become one of Italy's most visited museum sites, providing a singular experience for travelers. Going to Pompeii is to step back 2,000 years in time, where you will see old temples, theaters, and much more.

What to DO in Pompeii

Pompeii may seem like a small region, but it's not! It spans over 44 hectares, so if you intend to spend more time here, expect that it should take around two days to see everything; however, in the essence of saving time, this section will highlight some of the spots that are worthwhile seeing and something that should take no more than a day!

Regarding tickets and pricing, it's different in Pompeii, as there is one type of ticket (general admission) to access most of the sites (unless otherwise noted). The general admission cost for adults is €16; visitors under 18 get free admission, and all tickets must be booked online.

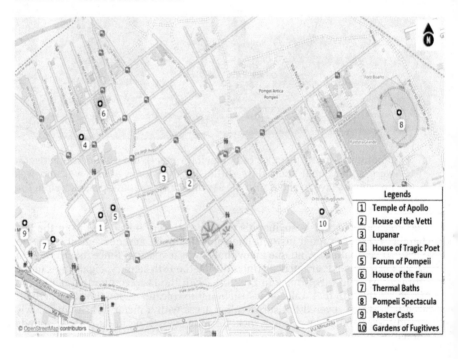

Sanctuary of Apollo

Pompeii is home to the oldest place of worship, the Sanctuary of Apollo. In Greek

and Roman Mythology, Apollo is the God of the Sun. The Romans worshiped Apollo as his God-like abilities helped them care for their animals and crops.

The Sanctuary of Apollo in Pompeii was believed to have been created by the Romans to honor Apollo in the sixth century B.C.E. Historians based their knowledge on the pottery fragments in Etruscan bowls from the same century. The remaining columns, walls, basins, and statues depict how grand the Sanctuary of Apollo was. As you look closer at the columns, you'll see carvings along some sections. You'll also see other interesting features, including an altar.

House of Vettii

The House of Vettii is an example of what a home looked like in ancient Rome. It

was one of the wealthiest and most famous houses in Pompeii and was protected by Priapus, the God of Prosperity, as seen in a painting to the right of the door. The owners of this house were two brothers: Aulus Vettius Restitutus and Aulus Vettius Conviva Liberti.

This house gives historians and tourists a detailed look into Pompeii's transition during the mid-first century. Following an earthquake, many Pompeii residents moved out of the area, allowing the "nouveau-riche" to rise and pursue stature and power. The Vettii brothers were a great example of new money as they rose from being slaves to rich merchants. Historians believe that when the brothers were bringing in fortune, they were able to purchase their prominent rank.

In addition to the rise of the nouveau-riche, there was a substantial decline in the well-being of others and moral standards. The house contains several graphic sculptures and paintings of an erotic nature, primarily focused on women being sexual objects.

Some other features of the house include heavily decorated rooms that overlook the atrium, including statues of cupids carrying out several activities, including wine selling, cleaning clothes, growing flowers, making jewelry, and making perfumes.

Lupanar

Hours of operation: 9 a.m. to 5:30 p.m. daily

Lupanar was an official brothel in Pompeii—and yes, it was legal! The brothel was visited daily by large numbers of men, given that Pompeii was a trading town.

Lupanar, a two-story building sitting between the north and south business districts on Via dell'Abbondanza, was excavated in 1862 by archaeologists. At the time the brothel was in business, it serviced Roman men who bought sexual favors from men and women prostitutes.

Lupanar has two floors: the apartments for the owner and prostitutes were on the upper level, while the five rooms for the services were on the lower level; every room had a built-in bed. Throughout Lupanar, you will see some paintings displaying erotic scenes and explicit graffiti where former clients expressed their options for the brothels and how the prostitutes performed.

House of the Tragic Poet

Hours of operation: 8:30 a.m. to 7:30 p.m. daily. The House of the Tragic Poet is a

typical house you would have seen during the Roman era, built around the second century B.C.E. This house is famous due to a collection of elaborate mosaics and frescoes depicting Greek mythology. Ever since the house was excavated (between 1824 and 1825), it has attracted the interest of academics and writers. The artworks and mosaics throughout the house were some of the best to be found in Pompeii. There is little known about the family who lived here, but it is worth the trip, especially to see the mosaic warning people to "beware of the dog" (*cave canem*).

Forum of Pompeii

Excavated in 1813, the Forum of Pompeii (or the Civil Forum) was Pompeii's core

for the city's daily life and the focal point for several buildings, including the main hall and commercial and religious organizations.

The square was originally an open area with a traditional rectangular shape made with clay. The eastern side contained shops, whereas the western side led to the Sanctuary of Apollo. Some notable buildings you will see in Pompeii's Forum include Temple of Jupiter, Arch to Drusus, Arch of Germanicus, Basilica, Several municipal buildings, Comitium, Eumachia, Macellum, Sanctuary of Lari Pubblici, Forum Granary, and Temple of Vespasian.

House of Faun

Hours of operation: 9 a.m. to 5: 30 p.m. daily

The House of Faun is one of the largest and most expensive houses in Pompeii, spanning about 30,000 square feet (basically the side of a city block). The house was home to an elite family (though it's unknown who) and was built sometime in the late second century B.C.E. As you'll see throughout Pompeii, the House of Faun contains several mosaics covering the floors (some are also on display at the National Museum of Naples).

Since the house's original construction, some changes were made to it over 250 years, but for the most part, it remained pretty much the way it was constructed until Mount Vesuvius erupted.

Interestingly, a mosaic version of a welcome mat with the Latin inscription "*have*," which also means "Hail to you!" is in front of the house. This welcoming mosaic was put together in Latin, suggesting the house was built before the Romans colonized Pompeii. You will also have the chance to see the door, framed by pillars decorated in capitals, and an entrance floor inlaid with yellow, green, red, and pink marble triangles. While we may never know the full spectrum of the family living here all those centuries ago, it's a fantastic house to wander through.

Pompeii Thermal Baths

Thermal baths were located throughout Roman cities, so naturally, Pompeii had some. The Pompeii Thermal Baths were the public baths in this area (before Mount Vesuvius destroyed them)—remember, bathing houses served as a place for people to bathe and socialize.

Pompeii's thermal baths had several facilities, including rooms to exercise in,  change, and hot- and cold-water rooms. The baths were heated underground using furnaces (just like the ones in Rome at the Baths of Caracalla), and a nearby trough supplied the water. As you walk through the baths, you'll see that they were intricately decorated with ornate decorations and artwork to display the level of Roman engineering and architecture. This bathhouse is so well preserved that it gives visitors valuable insight into the daily life and culture of the time.

Pompeii Amphitheater

Pompeii's amphitheater is the oldest known from the Roman era. It was built in 70 B.C.E. by Marcus Artorius Primus, just before the Roman colony was formed. The amphitheater held up to 20,000 spectators from Pompeii and the neighboring towns who came together to watch circus shows and gladiatorial games.

What you will notice with this amphitheater is that it does not have an underground area like others. Instead, it had a velarium to cover the arena in the rain. The rings that helped the velarium stay in place are still there.

Villa dei Misteri

Just outside Pompeii, on the road leading down to the harbor, lies a mysterious

villa called the Villa dei Misteri. The name came from a hall of mysteries in the residential section of the building. Walking along the hallway, you will see well-preserved frescoes spanning across three walls depicting a mysterious rite reserved for devotees of the cult of Dionysus, God of Decadence; the paintings show a woman who is being accepted into the cult.

Plaster Casts

Imagine what it was like when the civilians of Pompeii were going about their day

before Mount Vesuvius erupted. We'll never know what that fateful day was like. But we do have the opportunity to see the aftermath. As eerie as it sounds, stay with me.

When archeologists began excavating Pompeii, they started to uncover skeletons in the ash—but there was a void. Using plaster, they poured the mixture into the void, showing the final moments of the victims' lives. During the eruption's initial phase, many who hadn't left Pompeii in time were trapped in their homes, eventually being killed by pumice stones raining down or by roofs and walls collapsing due to the weight of the volcanic debris. In the second phase of the eruption, a high-temperature pyroclastic flow hit Pompeii and filled in the spots that did not have debris. The skeletons of the victims stayed in the same position, becoming calcified in layers of ash and preserving their bones (even after the rest of their bodies decomposed).

You can see these casts throughout Pompeii, the Archaeological Museum of Naples, and the Garden of Fugitives.

The Garden of the Fugitives

At one point, the Garden of Fugitives was a place for homes and, at another point, a vineyard. However, in the wake of Mount Vesuvius's disastrous eruption, the people of Pompeii had little time to react. The Garden of the Fugitives is where 13 victims tried to escape its pumice stone and other volcanic debris through the Nocera Gate. Unfortunately, they didn't make it when the pyroclastic flow entered. You can see the casts of the 13 victims near the garden's back wall.

Things to Experience and Enjoy in Pompeii

On the ruins of Pompeii, there are many ancient areas to discover to enhance your understanding of a time that was much before ours. However, despite it not being traditional in the sense of museums and such, you may be asking if there is anything you can experience and enjoy here, and there indeed is!

Take a Guided Tour or Tour on Your Own

The nice thing about joining a guided tour is that you have someone well-researched and knowledgeable on specific topics and the history of various places. The downside is that you're tied to their schedule and the group, leaving you less time to wander and explore independently. Whichever way you decide to tour Pompeii is your call! I love guided tours because if I have questions, they can answer them. But I also enjoy having the flexibility to explore on my own.

If you plan to do your own tour of Pompeii, it's a good idea to be prepared for your self-guided tour. As I said, you can tour Pompeii in two days, but it is vast, and you may not see everything. That said, the site is also not well marked, which could make it challenging to understand and appreciate the ruins you see.

If you decide to go on a guided tour, ensure you choose one with a qualified archaeologist. Your guide will navigate you through Pompeii, showing you the points of interest and the stories behind them.

Visit Herculaneum

There is a heavy focus on Pompeii, and how Mount Vesuvius destroyed it, so many

people forget about Herculaneum. Herculaneum is northwest of Pompeii and one of the better-preserved sites filled with crumbling buildings and artifacts—it was accidentally uncovered in 1709 when a well was being dug out; excavations did not officially start until 1738.

The name Herculaneum is believed to be related to the famous Greek god, suggesting the town was of Greek descent. At the time, the town was a prosperous coastal village and a tourist vacation spot for wealthy families. Herculaneum was initially spared Mount Vesuvius's debris, including the toxic gasses released from the volcano. However, its eruptions eventually caught up to Herculaneum. In 1981, some 300 skeletons were found scorched in boathouses and a moat.

Herculaneum is significantly smaller than Pompeii, making it easier to explore—it should take you no more than three hours!

Pompeii Food and Wine Tasting

Some places in or near Pompeii offer ancient Roman food and wine tours. In these 90-minute experiences, you can try delicious cuisines and sample different wines to transport you back to the ancient Roman period. You will also learn about the typical dishes, bread, and wine-growing culture.

Virtual Reality Experience of Pompeii's Reconstruction

Do you want to immerse yourself in Pompeii's history physically? Technology has allowed us to do just that with a virtual reality experience of Pompeii! A virtual reality tour of Pompeii will have you walking through reconstructions of the main site with VR equipment, allowing you to see the city before the volcanic eruption. It's different but entertaining!

Staying in Pompeii

If you plan a visit to Pompeii and want to stay as close to it as possible, several options are available. However, you can stay in Naples instead of changing hotels every few days. Naples has train services available to take you to the site and back. These are some suggestions for staying near the site:

Pompeii Ruins De Charme B&B: The Pompeii Ruins De Charme B&B is an excellent place to stay; it's 9.9 miles from Pompeii's site. This bed-and-breakfast has a balcony and a seating area and offers breakfast on-site.
Love Inn: The Love Inn is 10 miles from the ruins and offers a car rental service for your convenience (especially if you want to go to Mount Vesuvius). This inn has a shared lounge and terrace, which you can enjoy after a day of adventures. They also offer breakfast.
Vemaga Luxury Stay: If you want a more luxurious place to stay, check out the Vemaga Luxury Stay. This hotel is close to Pompeii's ruins and has a terrace and a shared lounge. They also offer bicycle and car rental services.

What NOT to Do in Pompeii

Pompeii is a different experience altogether, so avoid some of these things there! (Especially since this site is ancient and has some of Italy's most profound and richest history.)

Don't Climb on the Ruins or Walls
Although this tip is common sense, it's good to keep in mind that Pompeii contains delicate ancient ruins. By staying off the ruins and walls, you help preserve them for the future enjoyment of others and archaeological research efforts.

Don't Underrate the Size of Pompeii
If you intend to see various sites in Pompeii, doing it in one day is impossible as the site is large. Pompeii covers nearly five square miles, and before the volcano eruption, it was home to around 10,000 residents. Even if you take a tour, you won't see everything, but also be prepared to spend a whole day walking.

Don't Expect to Enter at Closing Time
Unless I have otherwise noted, Pompeii closes at 7:30 p.m. between April and the end of October and then at 5:30 p.m. between November and the end of March. Pompeii will stop selling tickets two hours before closing time, so don't be that person buying a ticket as they are finishing the day expecting to gain access.

Don't Feel Obliged to Join a Guided Tour
You have a few options for touring Pompeii and don't need to join a guided tour. As I said earlier, it's an excellent option to enhance your understanding of the various sites, but it's not required. Sometimes, adventuring on your own and learning things is more personal to you.

Don't Be Surprised by Lupanar's Artwork
Given that Lupanar was a brothel at one point don't be too surprised by the erotic artwork. In the historical sense, it was interesting that some of the artwork and graffiti were a form of communication between the customers and prostitutes.

Don't Expect Pompeii to Be Accessible
If you are a traveler with mobility issues or are traveling with some youngsters who need a stroller, Pompeii is not accessibility friendly. You can expect plenty of cobblestones, steep pathways, high curbs, and uneven pavement making it challenging. It's best to chat with a tour guide who can help you find the more accessible areas within Pompeii. That said, it might be better not to bring a stroller with you and instead use a baby carrier.

Remember, Pompeii Is an Active Site

Pompeii is busy daily with students and archeologists working to excavate and preserve Pompeii. Chances are you may come across some roped areas—don't cross them if you do! Additionally, it was the final resting place for thousands when the volcano erupted, so be mindful of this.

Don't Expect Plenty of Food Options

Compared to some of the other places in Italy, Pompeii has few options for food. They have a cafeteria, but it's better to bring your lunch and snacks! Also, don't forget to bring water as there is no place to buy water within Pompeii.

Don't Bring Large Bags

Large bags and backpacks are not allowed in Pompeii, so have something smaller to carry things in.

Remember to Grab a Map

Given the size of Pompeii, you want to make sure you have a map. Maps can be purchased at stalls in Pompeii (not at the entrance). Alternatively, you can print one off from Google Maps.

Pompeii is a fantastic site in Italy for many reasons, as you have learned throughout this chapter. No one would have known or learned about ancient life here had it not been for a tragic natural disaster thousands of years ago. However, the work and research of hundreds of archeologists have helped millions of people learn about a culture that existed before we could even imagine life.

In the next chapter, we will stay on this coast in Italy and check out another area that is relatively close to Pompeii, the Amalfi Coast.

Chapter 10

Amalfi Coast—Dos and Don'ts

If you're looking for another beach area to vacation in Italy, the Amalfi Coast (Costiera Amalfitana) is an excellent spot to achieve this! It is the definition of paradise with its 13 seaside towns, turquoise waters, and stunning, sky-high coastal cliffs displaying a vibrant skyline.

The Amalfi Coast also has some other notable parts about it. Along this coast, lemons are grown, and Italy's famous liquor, limoncello, is made. In addition, the Amalfi Coast became the backdrop of the fictional hometown of Wonder Woman—in the movie, the town was called Themyscira. This beautiful area is a breathtaking place to visit and stay in. So, let's look at what you should explore and discover in this coastal region.

What to DO on the Amalfi Coast

The Amalfi Coast can remind many of Cinque Terre, with its houses spilling down the cliff toward the ocean's blue watered edge. This coast is set in the southernmost part of the Sorrentine Peninsula, between Naples and Salerno, running for about 34 miles. As I said at the start of this chapter, there are 13 towns along the coast, all quaint and picturesque in their unique ways.

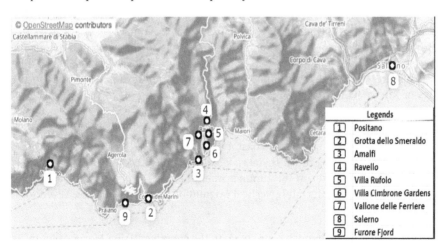

Amalfi

The Amalfi Coast's lavish beauty is one of the most famous in the world, with its

tall mountains in the distance and turquoise-colored sea. It's one of Italy's oldest maritime republics, succeeding under the Normans, Longobards, and the Saracens for three centuries until its decline in 1137 when the rival republic, Pisa, defeated and pillaged the coast.

Despite its history between successors, Amalfi became the town's expansive trading relations in the Mediterranean. More interesting is that the Amalfi-born scientist Flavio Gioia, was the one to invent the nautical compass.

Traveling to Amalfi, whether by sea, plane, or car, is an unforgettable experience for all travelers. There are several multiday packages you can look into to tour the coast, depending on how many days you intend to spend there. However, spending at least five days here is recommended to visit the most famous towns and the lesser-known hamlets.

Positano

Positano is the first town on our coastal tour and is one of the most popular towns to visit as it is a resort town. If you're looking to escape crowds (especially if you are coming to this area in the summer months), this is not the town to do it in. However, given its interesting vertical orientation, it is a place to see (even for a day).

While you are in Positano, be sure to go to the church of Santa Maria Assunta, as it has a beautiful dome with blue, green, and yellow majolica tiles. If you want to spend a day at the beach, Marina Grande Beach is a famous one to go to—you may even see some celebrities here! Over at Fornillo Beach, you can use snorkeling gear

and look at the gorgeous seabed. There are so many things to do in this little town, but it is one area worth spending even a day in!

The Emerald Grotto

Hours of operation: 9 a.m. to 3 p.m. daily; on Mondays, the Emerald Grotto is open from 9 a.m. to 2:30 p.m.

Imagine hearing about a mysterious cave where the waters were an emerald color, but no one had any proof. That was precisely what the Emerald Grotto (Grotta dello Smeraldo) was—a legendary (and likely nonexistent) grotto with seemingly magical colored waters. This legend remained among the locals until 1932, when fisherman Luigi Buonocore accidentally came across the cave.

The Emerald Grotto naturally formed over the centuries. When the sunlight filters through underwater openings, the light turns the water emerald, sending glittery reflections along the cave walls.

While the cave is gorgeous, it plays an important part in biodiversity as it houses many rare species. As you move through the cave, you'll also learn about the underwater ceramic nativity scene. Every year around Christmas, divers will place flowers around the scene.

If you want to visit the Emerald Grotto, you can do so by land or sea. If you're going by land, there is a small parking lot along the SS 163 highway (which connects all of the seaside towns in Amalfi Coast), and take the elevator or stairs down to the grotto's entrance. If you don't want to go by land (or you don't have a car), you can book a private transfer or join a private driving tour. Alternatively, if you go by sea, you'll buy a ticket and board one of the small rowboats for a guided visit (around 30 minutes long). If you are going the sea route, you can take a boat that departs from the Pannello Pier (however, this cost does not include admission to the cave).

If you're going to the Emerald Grotto, summer is the best time to go; however, be mindful that going on a weekend or during August will be busier.

As this is a cave, it may be closed without advanced notice due to bad weather or sea conditions. Here is the pricing breakdown:

Ticket Type	Cost
The Emerald Cave admission	€7 per person
Boat ride	€10 round trip (Remember: this does not include the cost of admission.)

Ravello

About 1,150 feet above sea level is one of Amalfi Coast's villages, Ravello. Ravello

gives you stunning panoramic views of the coast, which has earned itself the nickname the "balcony of the Amalfi coast."

The village is on a settlement site believed to have been built by a Roman colony escaping the Barbarian invasions. Ravello became a chosen refuge for some Amalfi noble families who rebelled against the authority of the Doge in the ninth century. The town managed to prosper when the Celendra wool production began, in addition to nominating its own duke for an attempt to disband its connections with the Maritime Republic of Amalfi. Ravello, unfortunately, faced a decline during the Norman Conquest, and its population subsequently began to diminish. However, despite its hardships throughout the centuries, Ravello always retained its charm and eventually became the destination for those seeking inspiration from every part of the world. For so many, Ravello is a dream.

Villa Rufolo

Hours of operation: 9 a.m. to 7 p.m. daily. Admission fees: €6 for adults, €5 for children between 5 and 12 years old, and for visitors 65 and up. Children who are under 5 get free admission.

Within Ravello is a house called the Villa Rufolo, with a tower overlooking the Piazza Vescovado, the heart of the village. The villa was commissioned during the medieval era by the Rufolo family, who were wealthy and powerful.

As you enter the house, be sure to climb to the top of the Torre Maggiore (past the entrance tower) to view the stunning sights of the Gulf of Salerno. As you walk through the house, you'll see some wonderful gardens awaiting you with beautiful flowers, lime trees, and Moorish architecture. If you happen to be here in July, the Villa Ruffalo hosts the Ravello Music Festival.

Villa Cimbrone

Hours of operation: 9 a.m. to 7 p.m. daily

The Villa Cimbrone was once an abandoned farmhouse. However, Lord William Beckett had a vision for the farmhouse. He purchased the farmhouse in 1904 to transform it into a beautiful residence, using a fusion of architectural styles and eras and decorating it with archeological artifacts and souvenirs from his travels.

Many travelers love coming to the Villa Cimbrone because it has a beautiful terrace called the Terrace of Infinity (Terrazzo dell'Infinito). The house has since been transformed into an exclusive hotel, so you can't wander through Lord William Beckett's former work, but you can still wander through the gardens and access the terrace to see the stunning views. As you are on the terrace, breathe in the stunning scents of wisteria, admire the statues and temples along the pathway, and stop to smell the roses in the rose garden. A tea room in a Moorish-style gazebo is also

decorated with Roman sculptures and columns, and it's a beautiful place to sit and take a long break. Admission into Villa Cimbrone is €7 per person.

Valle delle Ferriere

The Valle delle Ferriere is a unique adventure for those who love exploring beyond the beaches. Valle delle Ferriere is a beautiful area in a lush forest between the Lattari mountains of Scala with fern-lined streams. This area is neat because it has many physical and biological characteristics that keep rare plant species from distant eras alive. One of these plants is from the preglacial era: the Woodwardia radicans.

You can easily access the Valle delle Ferriere by foot—even if you aren't much of a hiker, you'll find the trails pleasant. Additionally, the vegetation and coolness of the forest are both stunning and refreshing, thanks to the streams and waterfalls in the area. It should take about three to four hours to hike the trail (around 3.4 miles).

Salerno

The province of Salerno is another small town overlooking the Tyrrhenian Sea, bursting with rich history, stunning landscapes, and natural realities. An earthquake hit this region in 1980, but it was restored, and much of its medieval structures miraculously remained intact during the event. Some notable places to visit in Salerno include

- Salerno Cathedral, built by Robert Guiscard, a Norman prince
- Church of Annunziata and its beautiful Baroque bell tower
- Church of S. Pietro a Corte
- Archi Castle

- Piazza Flavio Gioia
- Pinocchio Park
- Minerva Gardens

In addition, Salerno has plenty of green spaces to enjoy and have a picnic in.

Additionally, if you love hiking, you can walk along the Paths of Gods, a scenic route between Agerola and Positano. You may also want to check out the Cilento National Park and Vallo di Diano e Alburni for other outdoor hiking adventures.

Furore Fjord

Often referred to as the nonexistent town due to its lack of a main square and town

center, the Furore Fjord is a *ria*, a type of "coast with inlets where the sea penetrates" (*Furore*, n.d.a).

Based on geological confirmation, we now know that the Romans established Furore. It has always been an inaccessible area that even the Saracens couldn't invade. In some ways, it's kind of like J.M. Barrie's Neverland from Peter Pan and Wendy (Barrie, 1911).

When you are in Furore, you'll notice a suspension bridge hanging between two rock walls. In the so-called town, there are a few churches you can visit too, like Saint Elijah Church, Saint James Church, Saint Michael Church, and Saint Mary Church.

Bring your swimsuit to hang out along their cute little beaches! One thing to know about getting to this area is that cars aren't recommended, as there isn't much parking in the village. If you are driving, there is parking in Praiano, and then you'll hike 1.24 miles to Furore. Alternatively, public transportation from Salerno will take you to Furore.

Things to Experience and Enjoy on the Amalfi Coast

What do you do on the Amalfi Coast besides exploring some of the towns, hiking some trails, and enjoying the views? There are many things to explore and discover while on the Amalfi Coast. You can do plenty of things without breaking the bank to make your experience here unforgettable. This section will look at some of the experiences you should consider while planning your trip to the Amalfi Coast.

Take a Boat Tour of the Amalfi Coast

As you drive along the coast, you will be granted some beautiful views. This coast reminds me a little bit of Cinque Terre with its uniqueness (but of course, the difference is you can drive through here). And just like Cinque Terre, taking a boat ride to see the coast from the sea is an excellent option as it will give you a new perspective. There are a few ways to see the coast from a boat.

By Ferry

A ferry ride is the most cost-efficient way to see the Amalfi coast (and it makes it easier to get around in the summer to avoid the dreaded traffic jams). One thing to know is that not all towns are boat accessible. The ferry will only stop at these coastal towns: Sorrento, Positano, Amalfi, Salerno, Minori, Maiori, Cetara and Vietri sul Mare. A few companies offer ferry services, and each has its own schedule. They are Travelmar, Navigazione Libera del Golfo (NLG) and Alilaura Gruson.

Small, Guided Boat Tour

A small, guided boat tour is another cost-efficient way to tour the coast. Some of these boat tours can take the entire day, where they'll take you to various towns and sea caves, but there are shorter tours as well.

Private Boat Tour

One of the more expensive ways to tour the Amalfi Coast is on a private boat tour. On this tour, you can relax on the boat and see various small coves and caves that aren't accessible by ferry. Positano and Sorrento are two of the best spots to hire a private boat tour.

Taste Limoncello

As the Amalfi Coast is famous for its limoncello, it's nearly impossible not to see it

for sale at various shops (in addition to lemon-scented soaps and ceramics painted with lemons).

Limoncello has four ingredients: lemon peels, sugar, grain alcohol, and water. Limoncello is usually served cold, frozen, or as something to enjoy after dinner. Several shops will allow you to taste limoncello, and you can bring some home as a souvenir.

Try a Lemon Delight

Alongside limoncello, you can never go wrong with a tasty lemon treat. Lemon delights (*delizie al limone*) are a delicious treat. It's a cream-filled cake with limoncello topped with a generous layer of icing. It is both sweet and tangy, bound to light up your senses.

Spend the Day in Capri

Capri is another popular village among travelers, and it is one that you can spend a day in! This island has some unique natural features and is home to some animals and plants that only exist there. You will indeed be charmed by this vibrant town's mix of culture, landscape, art, and history. Some of the things you should do in Capri are

- taking a boat tour of the island.
- visiting the Blue Grotto (another cave with stunning blue, glowing water).
- taking a chairlift to the Monte Solaro to see some panoramic views of the area.

Take a Wine Tour of the Amalfi Coast Wine Road

Okay, I know I have mentioned wine several times throughout the book, but would it be an Italian trip if you didn't at least learn about the wine? Wine is a special piece of Italy, and being able to learn about their culture with it is always an enjoyable experience (as is even just seeing the vineyards).

On the Amalfi Coast, Tramonti is the main area of Amalfi's wine road. This route will take you past several vineyards along the hillside of the coast. As you visit these vineyards, you will feel like you're a part of the family, as much of the staff goes out of their way to make the experience memorable!

Hike the Sentiero degli Dei

Sentiero degli Dei (in English, this translates to the paths of the gods) is a beautiful walk high above Positano and Praiano. It's one of the more popular hikes on the Amalfi Coast for its beautiful views.

The hike begins in Bomerano and ends in Nocelle, which is about 3.5 miles long. It's a relatively easy hike (with some moderate areas). Along the way, you'll see beautiful views, stunning rock faces, and ruins.

You should avoid doing this hike if you suffer from vertigo, as some of the trail climbs to higher altitudes. It's also better to tackle this hike in the cooler seasons (spring or fall), as there is not enough shade to hide and rest in when it's hot.

Staying on the Amalfi Coast

The Amalfi Coast is a popular destination for millions, especially with its hundreds of beaches. Finding where to stay in this region of Italy will depend on your travel style. Before you book accommodations, it's best to figure out which town suits your style and budget for your Amalfi Coast vacation.

Sorrento

Sorrento is Amalfi Coast's starting point and one of the more accessible towns to reach—which is both a blessing and a curse. Sorrento is the destination for many day trippers, so you can expect it to be busy during the day, but it will also quiet down in the evenings when the day trippers go off to their next place. Regardless, Sorrento is an excellent spot to stay if you want a place where many locals speak English and you're looking for a central location to make day trips to other parts easier. Here are some places to check out:

Sorrento Marida Rooms: The Sorrento Marida Rooms hotel is a budget-friendly accommodation, steps from several beaches. All rooms have a full kitchen and dining area for your convenience.
Casa Ela: Casa Ela is a mid-range property with double rooms and a two-bedroom apartment accommodating up to four people. This accommodation is close to Sorrento's main shopping streets and restaurants for your convenience. In addition, you can start your day with a full Italian breakfast at a partnering café.
Sorrento Central and Sea View Flats: This hotel is excellent if you are traveling with your family, as it has several apartments that can accommodate up to five people. This hotel is near the main square (Piazza Tasso) and is close to Leonelli's Beach.

Positano

Positano is a larger town on the Amalfi Coast, and it's one of the most gorgeous spots due to its brightly colored buildings on the hillsides, villas, and beaches. There are plenty of hotels to stay at in this section and several restaurants to dine in. Given its location, you can expect to pay a little more here, but many people love coming to Positano if they're celebrating something special. Here are some places to check out:

Exclusive Apartments Positano: This property is in the mid-range for budget purposes, but it is an excellent one if you are traveling with a family, as it can accommodate up to four people. The terrace has a spectacular view of the coast and is close to the beach.

Hotel Bougainville: Hotel Bougainville is another mid-range priced accommodation central to most things, including the ferry and the beach. Some of these rooms have views of the sea as well!

Ravello

Ravello has some of the nicest coast views and several beautiful gardens, making it quite enchanting to stay in. Remember that Ravello is above the coastline, so you will be limited in how you transport to, from, and around the area. The good thing is that it won't be as busy because it's a little more challenging to get to, which can make for pleasant accommodation if you love to unwind in a quiet area after a busy day. Here are some places to check out:

Maera B&B Ravello: If you are traveling with a partner, this is a great little place to stay. This bed-and-breakfast accommodation is near the city center. It's a gorgeous property with great city views, a restaurant, a shared lounge, a bar, a garden, and a terrace. They also offer a continental breakfast.
Al Borgo Torello: The Al Borgo Torello property has a beautiful garden-like oasis with stunning views of the Amalfi Coast. In addition, they offer a shared kitchen for your convenience. This property is about 1.24 miles from the city center.

Amalfi

Amalfi is located along the water, with Amalfi Drive running through the center of the town, making this region conveniently accessible by land and water. This region is significantly smaller than Positano, so fewer hotel options are available. In addition, Amalfi can become quite crowded when people arrive to spend the day in the town and on its beaches. However, if you stay here, you can explore the town earlier and later in the day before the busyness comes and goes. Here are some accommodations to check out:

Holidays Baia D'Amalfi: This budget-friendly accommodation has some uniquely decorated rooms. They have a terrace overlooking the coast and are 130 feet from the beach.
Amalfitano Apartments: If you are looking for an apartment that can feel like your home away from home, the Amalfitano Apartments can check off these boxes. Each apartment has beautiful city views, a washing machine, and a fully equipped kitchen. In addition, this accommodation has a terrace, which would be a great place to enjoy your morning cappuccino!

What NOT to Do on the Amalfi Coast

With beautiful sea views and drool-worthy lemon trees, the Amalfi Coast is an enchanting place in Italy. But there are certainly some things that you should avoid doing to ensure you don't stand out like a tourist and your trip is enjoyable.

Don't Rent a Car
The Amalfi Coast may seem like a tremendous road-tripping spot, but some narrow, winding roads can create white-knuckle driving, especially in the summer when it's peak time for tourists. If you go to the Amalfi Coast during peak season, opt for public transportation, or if your budget allows, hire a driver. You'll save yourself the stress, and you'll be able to enjoy the views more! You will also save yourself the hassle of accidentally driving in limited traffic zones.

Don't Go in Peak Season
Summer is a prime time for everyone to travel, especially if they have kids out of school for a few months. Naturally, as more people learn about the Amalfi Coast, it draws them to the region, making it more crowded. If you are okay with not lounging on a beach, consider visiting the Amalfi coast during shoulder and off-season times. You'll be able to explore more quickly without it being crowded!

Don't Forget to Make Reservations
This tip was also mentioned in Chapter 4, but if you don't make reservations at restaurants between June and September, especially trendy ones, the chances of you getting a table are minimal. It's best to book seats as early as possible!

Don't Stick to Positano or Amalfi
While Positano and Amalfi have some picturesque hillsides and colorful homes facing the Tyrrhenian Sea, they aren't the only towns worth visiting while on the Amalfi Coast. You should also check out the less-crowded towns, such as Conca dei Marini and Ravello, as these towns also have spectacular views, and the hills are dotted with colorful buildings.

Don't Forget to Book a Boat Tour
If you want to see the Amalfi Coast on a guided tour boat or private boat, remember to book these in advance. These tours are inexpensive, and some may have stops along the way!

Don't Rely on the Ferry Service
Ferries can help you get around the Amalfi Coast, but some are only available between April and the end of October. Depending on when you are going to the Amalfi Coast, you may be unable to rely on the ferry service shuttling you to other places. In addition, ferry services could be canceled for the day if the weather or sea conditions are unfavorable.

Don't Forget to Rent a Beach Chair and Wear Water Shoes
If you want to have a beach day at any of Amalfi Coast's beaches, you will want to ensure you arrive early enough to rent a beach chair. You will notice that many beaches on the coast are pebbles, so it's not ideal to laze around on a beach towel.

In addition, because of the stones, I'd recommend wearing water shoes so that you don't hurt your feet trying to walk on the beach.

The Amalfi Coast is stunning in Italy, and you can see why many people flock here during summer! As you visit some of the seaside towns, you will see some stunning social media-worthy landscapes! While it might be tempting to spend a significant amount of time on the beach, make sure you give yourself the time to explore and experience certain parts of the coast, like seeing the shimmering emerald waters in the Emerald Cave and sipping on limoncello. No matter what you decide to do based on my recommendations (or maybe you have found some others), you will have a fabulous time on the Amalfi Coast.

You may also think the Amalfi Coast must be the tipping point for Mediterranean getaways in Italy, but you'd be surprised! There is another region that should go on your Italian travel bucket list. In the famous words of Sophia from the iconic sitcom *Golden Girls*, "Picture this, Sicily, 1922..." (*Golden Girls*, 1985).

Chapter 11

Sicily—Dos and Don'ts

A trip to Sicily (or Sicilia in Italian) offers every traveler a delightful vacation to the largest Mediterranean Sea Island. This Italian destination is well-known for its sandy beaches, but if you are a history buff, Sicily will feel like the ultimate educational island destination with its ancient ruins, baroque towns, and art. Sicily is also the place where the sonnet originated.

For outdoor lovers, Sicily is home to another active volcano, Mount Etna. Mount Etna is also a popular ski attraction (despite being an active volcano).

Given the region's positioning in the Mediterranean Sea, Sicily has been popular with explorers and researchers. In the 1940s, explorers located the Addaura Cave Drawings and proved that humans lived on this island 1.4 million years ago during Europe's Paleolithic era! When we think back to something like that, we most likely think about the dinosaurs that roamed the Earth, so to think of humans living this far back is crazy (cool)! There is so much more to discover and explore in Sicily.

What to DO in Sicily

There are not enough words in the dictionary to describe Sicily. That is

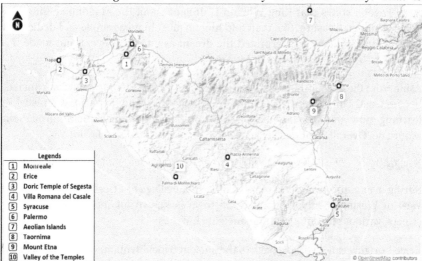

Legends
1. Monreale
2. Erice
3. Doric Temple of Segesta
4. Villa Romana del Casale
5. Syracuse
6. Palermo
7. Aeolian Islands
8. Taornima
9. Mount Etna
10. Valley of the Temples

© OpenStreetMap contributors

just how enchanting the island is. Between its rocky volcanic coastlines, white sandy beaches, architectural ruins, and well-preserved paintings from the Baroque era, there is much to marvel at while in Sicily. This small introduction is a sneak peek of what you should experience and discover while on the island.

Monreale

Monreale is a small hill town just outside of Palermo on the southwest slope of

Mount Caputo. The Normans initially founded the town in the 11th century. However, it grew more under King William II's reign when he took the throne in 1166. Legend states that King William II dreamt about the Madonna telling him about a hidden treasure. She then told him he must build a temple and dedicate it to her. King William II interpreted the dream as an actual event and made it a mission to build the Cathedral of Monreale.

Aside from the Cathedral, several narrow streets throughout Monreale and ancient houses exist. This town is also famous for its mosaics, and if you are interested in learning how mosaics are made, some craftsmen produce them throughout Monreale. Overall, Monreale is an excellent spot to spend the day in!

Erice

Sitting over 2,400 feet above sea level, the small village of Erice offers a bird's nest view of Western Sicily. This medieval town is known for its charming narrow streets, various stone houses, and ancient churches.

Erice's origins can be traced back to the ancient tribe, Elymian, who once occupied the western side of Sicily. It became known to the Romans based on a sanctuary atop a cliff dedicated to the Greek Goddess Aphrodite and Venus Ericina. The temple was a pagan temple, but as Christianity spread throughout the Roman Empire, the sanctuary fell into disrepair, eventually becoming destroyed.

Origins aside, Erice's history is rich, and its architecture is beautiful. There are 60 churches in the town, and if you happen to be here on a clear, sunny day, you can see the coast of Trapani. While you are in Erice, it's worth checking out the castles. One was transformed into a hotel (Pepoli), but the other, Venus Castle, is worth visiting. Venus Castle also has a beautiful garden to enjoy and soak up the views!

The Doric Temple of Segesta

The Doric Temple of Segesta is a must-see site in Sicily. Located in Segesta, the

magnificent temple is believed to have been built around 420 B.C.E. and is one of the most well-preserved Doric temples. What is funny about this temple is that it never appeared to be completed, though it's unclear whether or not this was on purpose. Further, the columns were not fluted (the shallow grooves you see in columns—think Greek columns), and the tabs used to lift the base's blocks remain. It leads to various theories as to why the temple was never completed!

You can see the Doric Temple of Segesta from Palermo's highway, but it's worth the detour to see it up close. There is no parking at the foot of the temple, but you can park and take a shuttle bus. The cost to park and take the shuttle is €5, and it covers the entire day. Here are the hours of operation throughout the year—the last time to be admitted to the area is one hour before closing:

Hours of Operation	
March 27 to September 30	9 a.m. to 7 p.m.
October 1 to October 31	9 a.m. to 6 p.m.
November 1 to February 28 or 29	9 a.m. to 5 p.m.
March 1 to March 26	9 a.m. to 6 p.m.

Villa Romana del Casale

Once the villa of a wealthy Roman family, the Villa Romana del Casale is filled with some of the best-preserved mosaics on the walls and floors. This villa was built in the fourth century and has over 38,000 square feet of mosaics in several colors, illustrating images of hunting, daily life, games, heroes, gods, and animals.

The villa has been divided into four sections, beginning with the enormous horseshoe-shaped entrance and its courtyard. From there, you'll move to the center of the villa, with a large fountain and 48 other rooms surrounding it. The mosaics have many themes, so take time to admire them before moving on to the next! Some mosaics may even surprise you with some forward thinking! To enter the Villa Romana del Casale, the ticket prices are as follows: Adults: €10, Visitors between 18 and 25: €5, and Visitors 17 and under are free.

Hours of Operation	
Last Sunday in March until the last Saturday in October	9 a.m. to 7 p.m. (last entry is at 6 p.m.)
From July 1 to September 30	9 a.m. to 11 p.m. (last entry is at 10 p.m.)
The last Sunday in October until the last Saturday in March	9 a.m. to 5 p.m. (last entry is at 4 p.m.)

Free entry days: first Sunday of every month, March 8, March 10, April 25, June 2 and November 4.

Syracuse

Visiting Syracuse is a trip back in time to a thousand-year-old city colonized in 745 B.C.E. by the Corinthians. What many love about Syracuse is that it is rich in

Roman and Greek history. This part of Sicily has some interesting architecture and the famous Greek Theater that dates back to the fifth century B.C.E. This arena is one the biggest globally, entirely mined from rock. It is still used today, but it's a fantastic place to sit and imagine the sounds of old performances from centuries ago.

Syracuse is also home to the Piazza Duomo, a stunning square—arguably one of the prettiest in Italy as Baroque palaces surround it and, of course, a cathedral. There are so many things I can list about Syracuse because there is so much to discover in this area! However, being here truly gives you a taste of ancient Greece and Rome together, and it is a remarkable adventure to be had.

Palermo

Palermo is the capital of Sicily and a busy area that may make you feel like you're

in a big city like New York with car horns honking nonstop. But it is a charming city with the delicious smell of baked goods, backstreets leading you to cute little squares, and churches decorated with colorful mosaics.

You won't fall short of some famous monuments left behind by several conquerors, including the Spaniards, Normans, and Arabs. Each one of these successors left their touch, adding to the heritage. Walking through the streets and seeing the scenic landscapes will undeniably make you feel like you're flipping through the physical pages of a history book! Additionally, Palermo has some excellent street food (more on that in the next section). Here are some places you should check out in Palermo: Baroque Palermo, Opera dei Pupi, and Catacombs of the Capuchins.

Aeolian Islands

You'll be left speechless when you see the Aeolian Islands. Seven main islands make the Aeolian Islands up (Vulcano, Lipari, Salina, Alicudi, Stromboli, Panarea, and Filicudi) in addition to five smaller ones (Lisca Newra, Dattilo, Basiluzzo, Bottaro, and Lisca Bianca).

There are some legends behind how the islands got their names, but it is connected to the Greek prince, Aeolus, who ruled a colony in this area. He could detect what the weather would do based on what one of the vapor clouds was doing above a volcano and the shape of the clouds in the atmosphere.

Some things you should do in this area include taking a boat trip around the

smaller islands, taking a donkey ride on Alicudi (as it does not have any roads), soaking in the sulfurous waters, and, if you are a rock climber, night climbing on Mount Stromboli.

Taormina

Taormina's nickname is the Pearl of the Ionian Sea, and you'll see why if you venture here! Taormina overlooks the turquoise-colored Ionian Sea from a natural terrace. In the distance, you'll see Syracuse and Mount Etna's summit, too! But

despite its gorgeous natural terrace allowing you to see Sicily from a different perspective, Taormina's history is fascinating, dating back to 358 B.C.E. when the Sicilians welcomed the Naxos, a surviving Greek Colony, onto their land. From there, this place grew, flourished, and saw challenges but continued to rise. People often holiday in Taormina to gain a taste of Greek history embedded in Italy. Throughout Taormina, you'll see cute villages, gorgeous beaches, and the Greco Teatro, the theater that gains plenty of attention and photographs.

Mount Etna

In the distance from Taormina and Sicily is Mount Etna, a stunning landscape with

desert areas, volcanic rocks, and thick, green forests. It is an active volcano that many tourists love to check out because it's the highest volcano in Europe. In addition, the landscape surrounding Mount Etna is incredible. It overlooks the Ionian Sea and the countryside lined with vineyards and groves.

The best way to explore Mount Etna is by joining a tour, which is either a half or full-day. These tours come from Taormina, Catania, or Messina. However, you can take a cable car up to about 8,200 feet and then join a guided hike or take a fun 4x4 Jeep ride!

Valley of the Temples

Atop a rocky ridge in Sicily lies the Valley of Temples, the most significant

archeological site globally. This temple is another Doric-style temple demonstrating Greek culture and art. This temple began sometime in the sixth century B.C.E. with the establishment of the Akragas colony. Akragas became a significant colony in Sicily when the Carthaginians lost to tyrant Theron during the Battle of Himera in 480 B.C.E.

The Valley of Temples covers 1,300 hectares. You should start your tour at the top

of Rupe Atenea, where you'll also enjoy the view of the archaeological site. From there, you can make your way down and see many of the temples standing there, including the Temple of Hercules, Zeus' Temple, the Temple of Demeter, the Temple of Juno, and the Temple of the Dioscuri.

Things to Experience and Enjoy in Sicily

One of the beautiful things about Sicily is how much archaeology is in this region. But beyond exploring Sicily, you should experience plenty of things while here, too!

Enjoy Sicilian Cuisine and Street Food

Of all the Italian food, Sicilian food is unique worldwide because it has a distinctive flavor. Sicilians don't even refer to their cuisine as Italian—everything is "Sicilian." In Sicily, you'll find world-famous foods, like cannoli, rustic Italian bread, and artichokes, and don't forget citrus-flavored things! Whether wandering through markets, sitting in a restaurant, or coming across one of the many street food vendors, be sure to try out some of their delicacies (your senses will thank you). Here are some of the delicacies I love and highly recommend trying:

Arancini (rice balls): Arancini are Sicilian rice balls, a beloved street food and

appetizer. Cooked risotto is rolled into balls and then filled with ragù (meat sauce), mozzarella, and sometimes peas. Coated in breadcrumbs and deep-fried to golden perfection, arancini offers a delicious blend of savory flavors and a crunchy exterior that delights food enthusiasts worldwide.

Pasta alla Norma: Pasta alla Norma is a flavorful Sicilian pasta dish featuring

tubular pasta, typically rigatoni, tossed in a tomato sauce with fried eggplant, garlic, and basil. The dish is then topped with ricotta salata, a salty, crumbly cheese, creating a delightful combination of textures and tastes.

Caponata: Caponata is a traditional Sicilian dish made with sautéed eggplant,

tomatoes, onions, olives, capers, and celery, all simmered in a sweet and sour sauce of vinegar and sugar. This delightful medley of flavors creates a savory and tangy relish, often served as a side dish or enjoyed on crusty bread as an appetizer.

Cannoli: consists of fried pastry shells filled with sweetened ricotta cheese, often

flavored with vanilla or citrus zest. Sometimes adorned with candied fruit, chocolate chips, or pistachios, these delectable treats offer a delightful crunch and creamy filling.

Visit Selinunte Archaeological Park

The Selinunte Archaeological Park is an expansive archeological site dating back to 600 B.C.E. At the time of its establishment, the area was populated by a large Greek colony that traveled from Megara Iblea. Today, it is recognized as the largest archeological site in Europe, where you can tour seven ruins of Doric temples and caves. It's a worthwhile experience, especially if you love hiking! The price of admission to the Selinunte Archaeological Park is €6. You can visit the park between 9 a.m. and 7 p.m. daily (with the last entrance time at 6 p.m.) unless otherwise noted.

Support an Anti-Mafia Tour

Italian Mafias are a topic everyone knows about, but they don't know much about it. The mafia significantly shaped Italy's culture, primarily in Sicily, and not in the best way. (Which, I mean, it's a Mafia—not a whole lot of good comes from these gangs for anyone.) Going on an anti-Mafia tour allows you to learn more about their culture and how they impacted Sicily and other regions in Italy, and you'll support their efforts to create a safer country.

Drive the Salt Road

Salt Road is along the coastline between Marsala and Trapani, surrounded by quaint windmills, beautiful waterfalls, ponds, and white salt pyramids. The first thing you'll notice while driving along this road is the contrast of colors between the yellow stones and blue sea, the green vegetation, and the white salt. It's a beautiful sight and so different compared to other places you'll see in Italy.

It's best to begin this excursion in Trapani by taking a tour of the harbor. You will see some colorful vessels and interesting architecture there, including the Tower of Ligny. This is also the ultimate place to watch sunsets. If you venture into Trapani's city center, the Cathedral of San Lorenzo overlooking the main street, Via Vittorio Emanuele, has a beautiful baroque exterior with impressive arches. In Marsala, you can visit an old mill, enjoy food at Trattorias, and see some beautiful salt pans (which makes for a great photo op).

Bask on the Beach

Sicily has some of the sandiest beaches in Italy, and the water is warm enough to wade and swim in for at least six months of the year. Some of the must-see beaches you should bask on are Caldura in Cefalù, San Lorenzo in Noto, Mondello in Palermo, Capo Bianco in Eraclea Minoa, Santa Maria del Focallo in Ragusa, Spiaggia dei Conigli in Lampedusa and San Vito lo Capo.

Drink Volcanic Wine

If you are headed to Sicily, going to a winery in Etna is a must due to the vines growing in volcanic-rich soil. These wines are earthy, savory, and a little ashy tasting, but the tart flavor will leave a lasting impression on your taste buds.

Staying in Sicily

Sicily is a favorite place for many to spend their holidays because you get the mix of ancient history tied to ancient Greece, an island with stunning turquoise waters, and plenty of places to adventure around the island. As always, where you stay will be based on what you want to do in Sicily.

Palermo

If you have never been to Sicily, you should stay in Palermo. In addition to a stunning landscape, Palermo is where you will see stunning baroque buildings, historical churches, plenty of museums, and art galleries. Here are some places to stay:

Hotel Mediterraneo: The hotel is a budget-friendly option near the harbor and Piazza Politeama, which is excellent if you are looking to join some guided tours.
Hotel Politeama: A more modern hotel built in the 1970s, Hotel Politeama is located in a historical and commercial part of town. Some rooms overlook bronze chariots in the nearby theater, the Politeama.

Cefalù

Cefalù is a great place to stay when traveling to Sicily with your family. It does not have wild nightlife or an entire tourist resort city, making it an excellent destination for little kids. Here are some options for where to stay:

Two Hearts Accommodations: Two Hearts Accommodations offers apartments near several points of interest, including Cefalù Beach.
Hotel Kalura: Hotel Kalura offers panoramic views of the bay and Rocca of Cefalù. This hotel has several resort amenities, including a pool and a tennis court.

Syracuse

If you stay in Syracuse, you will be within walking distance of various sites. You will find that most of the daytime activities center around historical buildings and museums. However, this area is also known for its nightlife. Here are some options to consider:

Alla Giudecca: Alla Giudecca is a beautiful hotel set in a 15th-century building. This hotel is gorgeous with its medieval accents and terraces.
Hotel Henry's House: This hotel overlooks the sea, offers a sun terrace, and most rooms feature a small balcony.

What NOT to Do in Sicily

Sicily is a beautiful spot to vacation in, but it's also not one to wander around in like a total amateur. Here are some things not to do while in Sicily.

Don't Underestimate Sicily's Size
Sicily is the Mediterranean's largest island, spanning about 620 miles wide. Many travelers underestimate its size and think they can do everything in three to four days—sadly, that's not the case. You need at least six days on the island to see the major spots!

Don't Make Mafia Jokes
Many Italian people, especially Sicilians, died at the hands of Mafias. Don't make jokes about the Mafia—it's disrespectful and insensitive.

Don't Only Pack for Hot Weather
While Sicily is in the middle of the Mediterranean and can get pretty warm during the day (don't forget your sunscreen), it cools off quite a bit in the evenings. Be sure to bring at least one sweater, jacket, and pants to keep you warm in the evenings when it dips to the 40s.

Sicily is one of the most enchanting islands you will ever see on this planet, especially with its rich ties to ancient Greece and its many different architectures throughout the region. Overall, Sicily is a fantastic lesson in history and a great place to relax. But do you want to take your relaxation mode to the next level? Italy's Lake District has several charming towns and lakes to relax and explore.

Chapter 12

The Lake District—Dos and Don'ts

W hen most people think about Italy, they immediately picture Rome's Colosseum, Tuscany's vineyards, and the Leaning Tower of Pisa. Many don't know (including myself at one point) that Italy has 1,500 lakes, ranging from small to massive. There are plenty of lakes and surrounding areas to explore, so let's get into it!

What to DO in the Lake District

Dispersed around northern Italy and near the Italian–Swiss border are many of Italy's lakes, surrounded by picturesque mountain backdrops, little towns, and more interesting Roman history. As you know, there are many lakes throughout Italy, so which ones should you spend your time in? I will recommend five of them as a must-visit location. They all are towards the north and north-east of Milan.

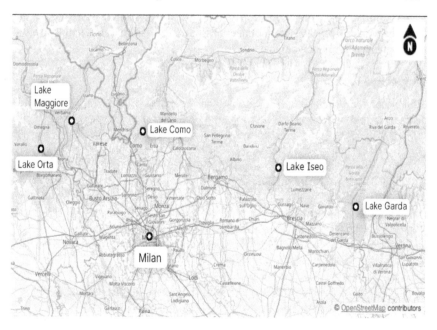

Lake Garda

Lake Garda is the largest lake in Italy, expanding across 143 square miles, with

several charming towns and villages scattered throughout its district. This beautiful area offers many things, including multiple historical sites, the Rivoli arena, and the Castello D'Arco, a castle on top of a hill.

Travelers who come to Lake Garda love to wander through the various towns and villages because of their colorful mosaics. The Peschiera del Garda is a neat place to check out if you want to explore a fortress town. Families also enjoy the Gardaland Amusement Park for some entertainment. On the water, you'll also see people kitesurfing and kayaking.

Lake Maggiore

As the second largest lake in the region, Lake Maggiore straddles the Switzerland

and Italian border on the south side of the Alps. This lake has a beautiful backdrop, thanks to the mountains. In the distance, you will see several small towns along the shores. People love setting out by boat to each of the main islands and soaking up the history of each town.

People who love nature particularly love Lake Maggiore because it has several botanical gardens. You will be amazed by the beautiful colors of the flowers and other plants.

Lake Maggiore is ideal if you also love to hike, and it's worth going to the National Park of Val Grande and the Natural Park of Ticino Valley!

Lake Como

Lake Como is a dreamy spot, with its villas and villages all surrounded by lush forests, mountains, and flower-filled gardens.

While in Lake Como, you don't want to miss seeing the Basilica di San Nicolò with an impressive 315-foot bell tower you can see from anywhere.

If you're looking for a place of ghosts, the Villa Pliniana has a fascinating story involving a forbidden love affair between Princess Anne-Marie Berthier and the Prince of Belgiojoso. They secretly wed, escaped, and found refuge on this village's shore, where they built an isolated life for nine years. Many believe the two lovers still walk the village and will jump into the lake at night with only a sheet.

You also cannot go to Lake Como without a tour of the town that gave the lake its name. Whatever you decide to do in Lake Como, you will find each day filled with new and unexpected discoveries!

Lake Orta

Lake Orta is one of the most underrated lakes in the Italian Lake District, possibly

due to its smaller size than Lake Maggiore. However, although the island is smaller in comparison, it has so many medieval buildings, adorable villages, and plenty of gardens it makes for a perfect family vacation.

One of the highlights of Lake Orta is the Isola di San Giulio (also known as the island of silence). This particular area has a functioning monastery. Here, it would be best if you visited a fourth-century Romanesque Basilica while taking a silent walk around the island. You'd be surprised by how therapeutic and meditative the walk is! Another highlight for literary lovers is visiting the charming village of Omega, where Italian writer Gianni Rodari was born. Rodari is best known for several Italian children's books and something that captures the attention of kids who come here.

Lake Iseo

Going to Lake Iseo will feel like you have stepped back in time with its well-preserved medieval buildings in their original layout, tower houses, and interesting alleyways. People love Lake Iseo for its shops, restaurants, and sporting activities!

In addition, there are some brightly colored buildings to catch your attention from land or sea.

History buffs and art lovers in town enjoy visiting places such as the Piazza Garibaldi. This square has several buildings surrounding it, including the Town

Hall and the church of Santa Maria del Mercato. There is also the 12th-century castle, Oldofredi Castle, which has an imposing stone structure towering over Iseo.

Lake Iseo is also an excellent spot for people who love nature, and you can find a great hike in the Torbiere del Sebino Natural Reserve. Whatever it is you are looking to do, whether it is to enjoy art, medieval buildings, water sports, or all of the above, you'd be surprised by what you can do in Lake Iseo, making it (and the other Lakes) a bucket-list item for your trip to Italy!

Things to Experience and Enjoy in the Italian Lake District

Now that you have learned about a few of the Italian Lake District islands and their lakes, what should you enjoy and experience while you are here? You should look into several experiences as the Italian Lake District can offer several opportunities for your entertainment and relaxation!

Explore Charming Towns

There are several charming towns, villages, and monuments to explore and learn about all over Italy. That's one of the amazing things about visiting other parts of the world, especially outside your country!

Lake Garda has many Baroque churches and the 12th-century fortress, now an art and history museum, allowing you to immerse yourself in a completely different world.

Lake Maggiore is one region that has historically attracted several famous people, including Queen Victoria and Winston Churchill. It has a dreamy appeal to it, especially along the lakefront. However, while you are here, visit the Villa Taranto to find thousands of plants and flowers. It's so beautiful!

Lake Como has a lot of buzz, considering actor George Clooney owns a house here. However, despite Lake Como being a hot spot for celebrity spotting, it's worth heading north to Tremezzina, where you'll see some small, beautiful towns and villas.

In Lake Orta, you will see why literary legends like Robert Browning and Lord Byron loved this region for the misty views and flowery backdrop. While in Lake Orta, walking through the cobblestone streets in the center is worthwhile as there are no vehicles. It will allow you to admire the town without the extra bustle!

In Lake Iseo, take the time to enjoy what living a lake-town lifestyle is like. The sights along the promenade are beautiful, and you can visit the nearby island, Monte, to see the different rustic hamlets and villages.

Water Sports

If water sports are something you love to do during the summer holidays, you don't need to head to a resort or beach to make this become a reality. Lake Garda and Lake Como are excellent spots to enjoy water sports. Both areas offer wind- or kite-surfing, wakeboarding, water skiing, diving, jet skiing, stand-up paddleboarding (SUP), kayaking, and canoeing.

Hiking, Cycling, and Nature Walks

One of the things I loved the most about the Italian Lake District was that there were endless places to enjoy the outdoors. Many people come to Italy, especially the areas along the Mediterranean, looking for a beach vacation combined with village excursions. However, coming to the Italian Lake District, especially in the autumn, is a great time to exercise your love of outdoor activities, such as hiking, cycling, and taking nature walks.

Hiking Trails and Nature Walks

You can see Switzerland across from Porto Ceresio, a little town in Lake Lugano (a district we didn't touch on)! There is a Cadorna Line hiking route that you should follow from the train station. Chances are, you'll come across people foraging mushrooms!

Lake Como has an old mule track called The Wayfarer's Way (Il Sentiero del Viendante) in Varenna. This trail will take you up some hills, and at the top, you'll be rewarded with a stunning view of the lake. The trail is about five miles from the neighboring town (Bellano), where you can catch the train back to Varenna.

The pretty town of Laveno in Lake Maggiore has the Sasso del Ferro Mountain hiking trail that hikers of any level can enjoy. This hiking trail will take you through gorgeous countryside and past villas and gardens. As you hike this trail, you will see gorgeous views of the Alps and the lake.

Cycling

Cycling around Italy is a great way to get around, and you can participate in some cycling tours in the Italian Lake District. Some are easy, while others are challenging, but the sites you get to see are worth it. For example, many tourists love to bicycle to the Madonna del Ghisallo—it has plenty of souvenirs, but the view of Lake Como is gorgeous.

If you are looking for a gentle cycling ride, many people enjoy Mantova for its scenes of ancient towers and domes. In addition, the pathway is flat to make the ride more enjoyable.

Gardens and Villas

The gardens and villas in the Italian Lake District create a dreamy and romantic setting for any traveler. They are so lavish, ancient, and beautiful that even those who don't have a green thumb can appreciate it. Here are some of the places that are most popular to visit:

Villa del Balbianello: Set on a high point near the village of Lenno, this 18th-century villa has some beautiful gardens. Interestingly, the Villa del Balbianello gardens have been featured in films such as *Star Wars: Episode II—Attack of the Clones* (Lucas, 2002) and *Casino Royale* (Campbell, 2006). Visitors to this villa can enjoy gardens that cling to the steep hills, topiary art, and an open-roofed gallery filled with statues while enjoying the views of Lake Como.
Sigurtà Garden Park: This garden park is located in Peschiera, Lake Garda, dating back to the 1400s. The Sigartà family owned this garden until the 1940s, and you can see the level of love and care that went into it then (and now). This park is about 148 acres and has a fun Labyrinth maze and a 400-year-old Great

Oak Tree. In addition, the current owners have a farm on the property with donkeys, sheep, and goats, making this garden park perfect if you are traveling with kids.

Villa Melzi: The Villa Melzi is in Bellagio on Lake Como. This location is an excellent spot to set up a blanket under one of the many tree species in the garden and read a book for a few hours. While wandering around the vast open green space, you will find several Egyptian and Roman statues, an orangery, and a Japanese garden with a fishpond and water lilies.

Isola Bella's Borromean Palace and Gardens: Isola Bella's Palace and Gardens is a 17th-century palace home to the wealthy merchant and banker family, the Borromeans. This dazzling palace has detailed rooms, several tapestries and paintings, and tiered gardens (which arguably steal the show). The gardens are on several terraces that lead down to Lake Maggiore and have fountains, statues, plants, flowers, and trees. When you look at the palace from the lake, it also looks like a ship!

Parco Arciducale: Parco Arciducale is in Arco, Lake Garda. It's more of an arboretum than a garden due to its many trees and shrubs. (About 200 different kinds, to be exact!) Lake Garda's relatively mild climate makes it easy to grow all types of trees and plants, some of which you would see in other areas like Asia and Australia! Parco Arciducale also has a lemon house that has several citrus trees. You'll learn a lot about plants while visiting this place!

Staying in the Italian Lake District

Of all the places in Italy, staying in the Italian Lake District is one of the most stunning places to wake up to. But where do you stay in such a gorgeous place? It all comes down to what you want to do and whether or not you wish to be in a more tourist-populated area.

Lake Garda

As Lake Garda is the biggest lake in the Italian Lake District, covering three Italian regions, it can be hard to decide where you want to stay based on your travel needs, especially since Lake Garda is a hot spot for water sports. Don't worry—I've got you covered with a couple of options:

Garda Life: If you have never been to Garda before, staying in the town of Riva del Garda is a must! The Garda Life hotel is budget-friendly with modern furnished rooms. It's conveniently located near the lakeshore and has a tour desk to help you with your tour needs.

Luxury Suite Sirmione: This hotel is located in Sirmione and is perfect for history buffs and beachgoers, as it is near several points of interest.

Lake Como

Due to its many little towns and villages, Lake Como is a popular tourist destination, whether it be people coming in from Milan for a day trip or intending to stay for a few days. Plenty of places will be right in the busy city center, while others will give you a relaxing vibe. Here are a couple of options to consider:

Miralago B&B and Apartments: Located in Bellagio, this accommodation is 10 minutes from the town's center. You can book a standard room or an apartment if you want to cook for yourself.

Hotel Royal Victoria: The Hotel Royal Victoria is in Varenna, which is perfect if you're not renting a car! This hotel is in a historic building a minute from the lake.

Lake Maggiore

Lake Maggiore is a picturesque place that is very close to Switzerland. There are several towns in this region, but I am a big fan of Cannobio for its small village energy and Verbania for its botanical gardens:

Hotel Elvezia: The Hotel Elvezia is in Cannobio and has beautiful rooms with high ceilings and a balcony! Guests are also welcome to relax in their garden or terrace; the lake is a minute away.

Hotel Pallanza: Located in Verbania, the Hotel Pallanza is a stunning hotel set in a 19th-century building with spacious rooms. This hotel is right on Lake Maggiore's shore and is near several boat connections to Stresa and the Borromean Islands.

Lake Orta

Lake Orta is one of the regions that is not overcrowded by tourists, which is good if you're looking for something more relaxed and less busy! Here are some places to consider staying at:

Hotel La Bussola: This hotel is gorgeous, with a pool backdropped by beautiful mountains. This hotel also has a garden with fun activities for you and your family's enjoyment.

Hotel Leon D'Oro: The Hotel Leon D'Oro is near the most popular square in Orta San Giulio and has a limited traffic area, making it more pleasant for walking around. They are on the water, so you can enjoy your meals while looking out at the lake.

What NOT to Do in the Italian Lake District

The Italian Lake District has many charming villages, towns, and scenery. At this point, there are many things you should remember not to do, including immortalizing yourself in historical buildings. We're going to keep this section simple!

Don't Expect Things to Be Open in Winter
The Italian Lake District is not the best spot to go to in the winter, and that's because most restaurants and establishments won't be open during those months. Don't expect things to be open if you plan to come here (even on a day trip)!

Don't Forget to Follow Local Regulations
While there are plenty of water sports you can do in the Italian Lake District, there are several rules and regulations surrounding them, especially regarding boating and jet skiing.

Swim in non-designated areas
While the lakes in the region may seem inviting for a swim, it's essential to follow safety regulations and swim only in designated areas. Some parts of the lakes might have strong currents or be unsafe for swimming.

Feed the wildlife
It may be tempting to feed ducks, swans, or other wildlife you encounter around the lakes, but feeding them human food can be harmful to their health and disrupt their natural behavior.

That said, if you go out and do water sports, make sure you keep yourself and other people safe while on the water! You don't want to cause an accident that could result in serious injuries.

The Italian Lake District might be the last chapter and place we're exploring for your trip to Italy, but words cannot describe how magnificent this part of Italy is. This area is amazing because it gives you so many picturesque views, charming medieval buildings, and places to hike and see the scenery from a different altitude. The Italian Lake District is a must for your travel bucket list! You won't regret it!

Conclusion

*C*ongratulazioni on making it to the end of the book! You have now attained so much knowledge of Italy that you should be able to start planning the trip of your dreams seamlessly! The point of this book was to help you find your path through Italy without feeling overwhelmed by the whole planning process, especially if you haven't traveled since the COVID-19 pandemic took over the globe in what seemed like seconds.

Italy is beautiful, as you have read throughout the book and seen some of the photos shared throughout. (And if you go online and Google "Italy," you'll see thousands of more stunning photos!)

As you plan your trip to Italy, remember when you want to go because this will impact your experience. If you go during the summer, expect it to be quite busy. If you go in the autumn, winter, or spring, it won't be as busy, making it better to go to various attractions. What you plan also goes into how you envision your Italy trip. What do you want to do while you are there? Do you want to go on several wine tours? Maybe you're going for the delicious food and to see the art galleries, museums, and historical landmarks. Those interests are tied to the season you plan to go to Italy.

As you begin planning your trip, consider the types of tours you want to go on. I know sometimes people can find guided tours boring, but joining other fellow travelers and learning from an expert can be fun! (And think of the memories and new friends you'll meet while on them.)

As for getting around Italy, public transportation is arguably your best mode of transportation. You'll save yourself the hassle of limited driving zones, tickets, and other headaches! Most of Italy has excellent public transportation, so utilize it as much as possible! Remember, if you plan to take a taxi, do not use your hands to flag it down (you'll look silly).

As you travel through Italy, be aware of your surroundings and potential scammers. Several people may try to distract you so they can pickpocket you (gypsies), or they may try to demand payment from you if they give you a friendship bracelet. Also, remember that while knock-off brands are enticing, they are illegal to buy and sell, so stay clear of those vendors!

Traveling to Milan

Milan has some of the most exciting pieces of history, especially with its various rulers throughout the centuries. But despite its rich history, Milan is a center for fashion and design, in addition to keeping its history close to its core. No matter what experiences and monuments you want to see, you will leave Milan feeling like you have been immersed in its elegance and art and being able to witness some of Leonardo da Vinci's greatness.

Traveling to Cinque Terre

The region of Cinque Terre is a beautiful spot to visit. It's incredible how five small villages can make up a national park. People are drawn here because of the houses on the hills. But that's not all that brings people to this region.

If you come to Cinque Terre in the summer, lounging around on the beach is a must! However, taking boat rides to see Cinque Terre from the water will allow you to see the vibrant colors of the buildings. Remember, though, Cinque Terre does not have pools or many shopping opportunities. It's also not a region you should try to squeeze everything in if you will only be here for a few days!

Traveling to Venice

Venice is a romantic city—ask anyone! The winding streets and canals are beautiful throughout this city, so taking a gondola ride (at least once) is worth the experience!

Venice has some fabulous architecture, rich in history. When you go to Venice, enjoy seeing places like the Rialto Bridge and the Grand Canal! It's also worth learning more about their mask-making since that's been a large tradition of this city for years.

While in Venice, remember they don't allow any cars in the city center. You'll be walking a good chunk of the time with many others.

Traveling to Tuscany

Tuscany is a whimsical territory, home to many famous people like Michelangelo and da Vinci! Tuscany's rich history, dating back 3,000 years ago, allows us travelers to step foot in some of the most iconic cities that made Tuscany what it is today. In addition, getting to see the rolling green hills and vineyards throughout is a treat for anyone. However, seeing some churches, such as the historic Florentine churches, will leave a lasting impression. And we can't forget about going to the Tower of Pisa (and yes, I empower you to take one of those fun photos of you "supporting" the tower).

Traveling to Rome

Rome is one of the first places most people think of when Italy comes to mind, and for a good reason. Going to Rome and seeing several famous sites, including St. Peter's Square and the Colosseum, is impressive. There is truly nothing like it on this planet. And maybe if you do toss that coin into Trevi, you'll get to come back to Rome again. Wherever you end up in Rome, allow yourself to be on an adventure here because its history is rich and exciting.

Traveling to Naples

There is so much more I want to say about Naples, but there are not enough words to describe how beautiful and unique it is—especially with its ties to ancient Greece.

In many ways, Naples is the starting point of a time capsule. It has so many archeological things to see and castles to admire. In the distance, you have an active volcano, a region people love hiking up and seeing. There is so much to see and do in Naples, especially with a city of its size. But make sure to take advantage of some of the things I recommended because they add a unique experience to your trip.

Traveling to Pompeii

Pompeii is a time capsule, stopping thousands in their tracks when Mount Vesuvius erupted suddenly. That is what makes Pompeii so interesting. So many ruins have created amazing archaeological sites, and people are still digging up artifacts today! Pompeii gives us a glimpse into a life well before we can fathom life existing, and it is one of the most exciting places to go to! This is one of the places where you don't need a guided tour because it's not that big. Pompeii is where you can make your discoveries (while respecting the work of archeologists) and imagine what life was like at that time.

Traveling to the Amalfi Coast

Moving away from Pompeii, the Amalfi Coast is another dreamy region with 13 seaside towns. The turquoise waters will surely leave you breathless.

Amalfi is the perfect spot to see a different way of living in seaside towns. However, it's also an excellent place to do some neat excursions—who would have thought that a cave could create the most beautiful emerald-green waters? When you are done exploring and experiencing different things in this region, be sure to sit back on a restaurant patio and sip on some yummy limoncello!

Traveling to Sicily

Traveling to Sicily takes you back in time for many reasons—some of it has to do with its ancient ruins, but you can also learn more about the Mafias and how they negatively impacted Sicily (and still do). However, despite its Mafia history, people are enchanted by Sicily because of its volcanic coastlines and white, sandy beaches. It's no wonder that Sicily seduces its visitors!

Traveling to the Italian Lake District

The Italian Lake District in Northern Italy gives you so many beautiful views. It's amazingly close to Switzerland, has so many charming towns throughout the district, and has many fun things to see and do. This is a perfect vacation spot for anyone who loves adventures!

As you plan your trip to Italy, unveil the secrets of this extraordinary country and create memories that will last a lifetime. And remember, as you delve into the wonders, keep the "what *not* to do" tips close to your heart, ensuring a truly authentic and respectful experience at every step. Start your Italian adventure today!

If this book has helped ignite your adventurous heart, please leave a review on Amazon.

Glossary

€: The symbol for the euro currency.
Amatriciana: A bacon and tomato-based pasta found in Rome.
Aperitivo: An aperitif to drink before dinner.
Arrivederci: Translates to "goodbye" in English.
Bankomat: An ATM machine.
Bene: Translates to "good" in English.
Buongiorno: A greeting to say "good morning" or "good day."
Buona sera: A greeting to say, "good evening" or "goodnight."
Carabinieri: A special Italian army branch.
Carciofi alla Romana: A traditional Roman pasta with artichokes.
Ciao: A way to say "hello" and "goodbye."
> **Special note:** Only use this if you know the person well. If you do not, use any of the other greetings noted in the glossary.

Cipollina: A street food made with sautéed spring onions, mozzarella, ham, and tomato sauce in a fluffy pastry crust.
Cucina profumata: Translates to "a fragrant cuisine" in English.
Farmacia: Translates to "pharmacy" in English.
Fontana dei Quattro Fiumi: The Fountain of the Four Rivers.
Fontana del Moro: The Moor Fountain.
Fontana del Nettuno: The Fountain of Neptune.
Fontana di Trevi: The Trevi Fountain.
Grazie: Translates to "thank you" in English.
Limoncello: An Italian liqueur made with lemons.
Mi dispiace or mi scusi: Translates to "my apologies" in English.
Non capisco: Translates to "I don't understand" in English.
Non parlo italiano: A way to tell someone that you don't speak Italian.
Parla inglese?: How to ask someone if they speak English.
Pasta alla carbonara: A traditional carbonara pasta found in Rome.
Pasta cacio e pepe: Pepper and cheese pasta dish found in Rome.
Per favore: Translates to "please" in English. (Use this when you are making a request.)
Piazza di Spagna: The Spanish Square in Rome.
Pidone: A Sicilian street food in a triangle or crescent moon-shaped pastry stuffed with anchovies, tuna, and curly endive fried for your enjoyment.
Prego: A duplicate way to say "please" and "you're welcome."
Salve: An informal way to say "greetings."
Sonnet: A poetic form of 14 lines following a specific structure rhyme scheme.
Zona traffico limitato: A limited traffic area.

References

Aeolian Islands. (n.d.). Visit Sicily. https://www.visitsicily.info/en/localita/eolie/

Airfare to Italy. (n.d.). Italy Explained. https://italyexplained.com/italy-travel-guide/airfare-to-italy/

Amalfi. (n.d.-a). Italia.it. https://www.italia.it/en/campania/salerno/amalfi

Amalfi. (n.d.-b). Positano.com. https://www.positano.com/en/e/amalfi

Amalfi Coast. (n.d.). Italy Magazine. https://www.italymagazine.com/amalfi-coast

Amir, O. (2022, February 27). *150 beautiful Italy quotes to ignite your wanderlust.* My Path in the World. https://mypathintheworld.com/italy-quotes-about-italy/

Amphitheater. (n.d.). Pompeii Sites. http://pompeiisites.org/en/archaeological-site/amphitheater/

Andreas. (2016, May 9). *Cycling the Italian Lake District.* London Cyclist. https://www.londoncyclist.co.uk/cycling-italian-lake-district/

Andrew and Emily. (2023a, April). *Thirteen wonderful things to do in Cinque Terre.* Along Dusty Roads. https://www.alongdustyroads.com/posts/things-to-do-cinque-terre

Andrew and Emily. (2023b, April). *An essential guide to Riomaggiore.* Along Dusty Roads. https://www.alongdustyroads.com/posts/riomaggiore-cinque-terre

Aperitif in Brera: 5 spots. (n.d.). FLAWLESS.life. https://flawless.life/en/italy/milan/aperitif-in-brera-5-spots

Aperitivo in Navigli: best bars on the canals of Milan • Milan by locals. (2023, February 2). Nosbatti. https://nosbatti.com/aperitivo-in-navigli-best-bars/

Automobile Club d'Italia. (2023, February 16). *Everything you need to know about driving in Italy: road rules, tips and useful information.* Italia.it. https://www.italia.it/en/italy/things-to-do/tutto-quello-che-ce-da-sapere-per-guidare-in-italia-regole-stradali-consigli-e-informazioni-utili#what-are-the-requirements-and-documents-necessary-for-driving-in-italy-

Barrie, J. M. (1911). *Peter Pan and Wendy.* Hodder & Stoughton.

Basilica of Saint Peter. (n.d.). Italia.it. https://www.italia.it/en/lazio/rome/st-peter-basilica

Baths of Caracalla. (n.d.). Rome.info. https://www.rome.info/attractions/baths-of-caracalla/

Baths of Caracalla. (n.d.-b). Civitatis Rome. https://www.rome.net/baths-caracalla

Bauso, A. O. (2019, May 6). *12 rookie mistakes to avoid on your Sicily vacation.* Oyster. https://www.oyster.com/articles/rookie-mistakes-to-avoid-on-your-sicily-vacation/

Beautiful gardens to visit in the Italian lakes. (n.d.). TUI. https://www.tui.co.uk/discover/best-gardens-visit-italian-lakes

Bensalhia, J. (2018, February 19). *A beginner's guide to the do's and don'ts of driving in Italy.* ITALY Magazine. https://www.italymagazine.com/featured-story/beginners-guide-dos-and-donts-driving-italy

Bernard, E., & Bisceglie, A. (2021, September 12). *What's so special about Roman cuisine? To me, a lot!* Romewise. https://www.romewise.com/roman-cuisine.html#what-is-roman-cuisine

Bertrand, E. (2022, December 31). *Italy's favourite summer festivals.* Dolcevia.com. https://www.dolcevia.com/en/italys-favourite-summer-festivals

Best gelato in Milan: artisanal Italian gelaterie you must try. (2023, March 4). Nosbatti. https://nosbatti.com/best-gelato-milan/

Boat tours. (n.d.). Naples Insider. https://www.naplesinsider.com/en/l/rent-boat

Bonadonna, E. (2022, December 14). *The carnival of Venice and its traditional masks.* Culture Trip. https://theculturetrip.com/europe/italy/articles/the-carnival-of-venice-and-its-traditional-masks/

Bond, S. E. (2019, October). *The brothels of ancient Pompeii.* History Today. https://www.historytoday.com/reviews/brothels-ancient-pompeii

Bounce. (2023, June 22). *Is Milan safe to visit? A comprehensive safety guide.* https://usebounce.com/guides/milan/is-milan-safe-to-visit

Brady, S. (2023, April 24). *31 ways you could get into trouble as a tourist in Italy in 2023.* Lonely Planet. https://www.lonelyplanet.com/news/what-not-to-do-as-a-tourist-in-italy

Brera. (n.d.). Italia.it. https://www.italia.it/en/lombardy/milan/brera

Brewer, S. (2023, May 19). *How to travel in Italy for cheap: 30 money-saving tips.* Frommers. https://www.frommers.com/tips/money-and-currency/how-to-travel-in-italy-for-cheap-30-money-saving-tips

Britannica, T. Editors of Encyclopaedia. (2023, March 8). *Pinacoteca di Brera.* https://www.britannica.com/topic/Pinacoteca-di-Brera

Burano Italy, a Venice's island. (n.d.). Isolsd Di Burano.it. https://www.isoladiburano.it/en/

Cameron, L. A. (2018, March 15). *Why you should get lost in Venice.* Venice by Venetians. https://www.venicebyvenetians.com/lost-venice/

Campbell, M. (Director). (2006). *Casino Royale* [Film]. Columbia Pictures.

Candice. (2022, October 25). *Italy packing list – tips and advice based on 20 years of experience.* Mom in Italy. https://mominitaly.com/italy-packing-list/#What_Not_to_Pack_for_a_Trip_to_Italy

Cappella Sansevero. (n.d.). Civitatis Naples. https://www.introducingnaples.com/cappella-sansevero

Capri. (n.d.). Italia.it. https://www.italia.it/en/campania/naples/capri

Carrick, E. (2019, March 19). *8 costly mistakes you're making when booking flights – and how to avoid them.* Travel + Leisure. https://www.travelandleisure.com/travel-tips/booking-mistakes-to-avoid

Casale, R., & Rhodes, E. (2021, July 14). *The best and worst times to visit Italy.* Travel + Leisure. https://www.travelandleisure.com/travel-tips/best-time-to-visit-italy

Castel dell'Ovo: history and magic between land and sea. (n.d.). Visitnaples.eu. https://www.visitnaples.eu/en/neapolitanity/walk-naples/castel-dell-ovo-history-and-magic-between-land-and-sea

Castel dell'Ovo. (n.d.). Italia.it. https://www.italia.it/en/campania/naples/castel-dell-ovo

Castel Nuovo. (n.d.). Civitatis Naples. https://www.introducingnaples.com/castel-nuovo

Catacombs of Rome. (n.d.). Civitatis Rome. https://www.rome.net/catacombs-rome?_gl=1

Cinque Terre. (n.d.). Italia.it. https://www.italia.it/en/liguria/cinque-terre

Cinque Terre ferry boat timetable and prices 2023. (2023, June 25). CinqueTerre.eu.com. https://www.cinqueterre.eu.com/en/boat-excursions

Cinque Terre National Park. (n.d.). Italia.it. https://www.italia.it/en/liguria/la-spezia/cinque-terre-national-park

Cinque Terre: enchanting villages overlooking the sea in Liguria. (2022, September 26). Italia.it. https://www.italia.it/en/liguria/things-to-do/porto-venere-and-cinque-terre

Claudia Tavani. (2023, January 8). *What to do and what to avoid when planning a trip to Italy.* My Adventures across the World. https://myadventuresacrosstheworld.com/planning-a-trip-to-italy/

Collodi, C. (1946). *The adventures Of Pinnocchio.* Groset And Dunlap.

Condie, L. (2015, January 14). *13 things not to do in Florence.* HuffPost. https://www.huffpost.com/entry/travel-to-florence_b_6128692

Corniglia. (n.d.). Best of Cinque Terre.com. https://www.bestofcinqueterre.com/en/corniglia

Corniglia. (n.d.). Italia.it. https://www.italia.it/en/liguria/la-spezia/corniglia

Corniglia. (n.d.). Italian-Riviera.com. https://www.italian-riviera.com/en/cinque-terre/corniglia

Correale, M. (2020, December 2). *The best town to stay in Cinque Terre: how to choose the perfect one | Mama Loves Italy.* Mama Loves Italy. https://mamalovesitaly.com/best-town-to-stay-in-cinque-terre/

Corrias, A. (2019, August 9). *Italy packing list – what to pack for Italy season by season.* Chasing the Unexpected. https://www.chasingtheunexpected.com/italy-packing-list/

Damiani, M. (2021, June 23). *Twelve do's and don'ts in Cinque Terre.* https://michelledamiani.com/travel-in-italy/twelve-dos-and-donts-in-cinque-terre

Dani. (2022, July 28). *Go beyond... Pisa's Leaning Tower.* GlobetrotterGirls. https://globetrottergirls.com/go-beyond-pisas-leaning-tower/

Dario. (2018, September 7). *A brief history of Venice.* Venice by Venetians. https://www.venicebyvenetians.com/brief-history-venice/

Deere, K. (2022, November 26). *Where to stay in Rome: an area by area guide.* Rough Guides. https://www.roughguides.com/articles/where-to-stay-in-rome-italy/

Dickerson, N. (2021, June 23). *Sicilian cuisine: culinary jewel of the Mediterranean.* Cellar Tours. https://www.cellartours.com/blog/italy/sicilian-cuisine

Discover Pompeii and its food and wine (n.d.). Visitnaples.eu. https://www.visitnaples.eu/en/neapolitanity/flavours-of-naples/discover-pompeii-and-its-food-and-wine

Dombrowski, J. (n.d.). *Wonder Woman's Themyscira actually exists.* Luxe Adventure Traveler. https://luxeadventuretraveler.com/wonder-woman-themyscira-filming-locations-italy/

Dowd, H. (2019, April 22). *How to exchange money for your trip to Italy.* Tourissimo. https://www.tourissimo.travel/blog/how-to-exchange-money-for-your-trip-to-italy

Duomo Di Milano. (n.d.). Italia.it. https://www.italia.it/en/lombardy/milan/milan-cathedral

EA Editors. (2020, September 7). *Why Italy is such a popular vacation destination.* Escape Artist. https://www.escapeartist.com/blog/italy-popular-vacation-destination/

11 fun facts about Venice (you probably didn't know). (2020, May 25). GetYourGuide. https://www.getyourguide.com/magazine/2020/05/fun-facts-about-venice/

Erice. (n.d.). Italia.it. https://www.italia.it/en/sicily/trapani/erice

Erice, Sicily; a beautiful hilltop village with stunning views. (n.d.). Sicily Visitor. https://www.sicily-visitor.com/places/erice.php

Evanson, N. (n.d.). *Learning to communicate with the locals in Italy – some tips for expats.* Expat Focus. https://www.expatfocus.com/italy/living/learning-to-communicate-with-the-locals-in-italy-some-tips-for-expats-1444

Evason, N. (2017). *Italian culture.* Cultural Atlas. https://culturalatlas.sbs.com.au/italian-culture/italian-culture-core-concepts

Everything you should know about Italian Customs and Etiquette. (n.d.). ItalianPod101.com Blog. https://www.italianpod101.com/blog/2020/01/06/italian-etiquette/

Ferry & boat tours around Lake Como. (n.d.). Lake Como Travel. https://lakecomotravel.com/boat-tours-ferry-lake-como/

Finzi, A. (2023, January 2). *The majestic rooftop terraces of the Duomo.* MILAN Welcome City Guide. https://milan.welcomemagazine.it/entertainment-experiences/the-majestic-rooftop-terraces-of-the-duomo/

Fisher, S. (2016, September 8). *4 fascinating & powerful anti-mafia tours in Italy* Epicure & Culture. https://epicureandculture.com/things-to-do-in-italy/

Fontana del Nettuno. (n.d.). Bologna-Modena Tourist Territory. https://www.bolognawelcome.com/en/places/squares-streets-monuments/fontana-del-nettuno-2

Foot, J., Cosgrove, D. E., & Cessi, R. (2023). Venice. In *Encyclopædia Britannica.* https://www.britannica.com/place/Venice

Forum. (n.d.). Pompeii Sites. http://pompeiisites.org/en/archaeological-site/forum/

Frey, L. (2023a, June 6). *The best time to visit Italy.* The Broke Backpacker. https://www.thebrokebackpacker.com/best-time-to-visit-italy/

Frey, L. (2023b, June 22). *Where to stay in Cinque Terre (2023 – the coolest areas!).* The Broke Backpacker. https://www.thebrokebackpacker.com/where-to-stay-in-cinque-terre-italy/

Furore. (n.d.). Amalfi Coast. https://www.infoamalficoast.com/furore/

Furore. (n.d.). Italia.it. https://www.italia.it/en/campania/furore

Galleria Borghese & Villa Borghese Rome. (n.d.). RomeSite.com. https://romesite.com/galleria-borghese.html

Game of thrones. (2011). [TV Series]. HBO.

Garden of the fugitives. (n.d.). Pompeii Sites. http://pompeiisites.org/en/archaeological-site/garden-of-the-fugitives/

Garrison, M. (2023, April 4). *Avoid making these 8 mistakes on the Amalfi Coast this summer.* Fodors Travel. https://www.fodors.com/world/europe/italy/experiences/news/things-not-to-do-on-the-Amalfi-coast

Golden Girls. (1985). [TV Series]. NBC.

Gondola ride in Venice, Italy. (n.d.). Venezia Authetica. https://veneziaautentica.com/gondola-ride-venice/

Grant, L. (2018, December 5). *8 rookie mistakes to avoid in the Amalfi Coast.* Oyster. https://www.oyster.com/articles/what-not-to-do-in-the-amalfi-coast/

Grotta dello Smeraldo. (n.d.). Italia.it. https://www.italia.it/en/campania/salerno/grotta-dello-smeraldo

Guide, R. (n.d.). *A guide to Palatine Hill: everything you need to know.* Roma Experience. https://www.romaexperience.com/post/palatine-hill

Hari. (n.d.). *Great things to know before flying to Italy.* ITALY IRL. https://www.italyirl.com/great-things-to-know-before-booking-a-flight-to-italy/

Henderson, J. (2017, July 18). *Our favourite Lake Orta locations.* ShuttleDirect. https://www.shuttledirect.com/blog/favourite-lake-orta-locations/

Hengel, L. (2017, June 14). *13 Things Tourists Should Never Do in Rome, Ever.* Culture Trip. https://theculturetrip.com/europe/italy/articles/13-things-tourists-should-never-do-in-rome/

Herculaneum (Ercolano), Italy. (n.d.). Sightseeing Tours Italy. https://www.pompeiitours.it/attractions/herculaneum/

Hirst, K. K. (2020, February 18). *House of the Faun at Pompeii – Pompeii's richest residence.* ThoughtCo. https://www.thoughtco.com/house-of-the-faun-at-pompeii-169650

History of Milan. (n.d.). Passepartout. https://www.passepartout-italia.it/history-of-milan/

History.com Editors. (2009, November 9). *Colosseum*. HISTORY; A&E television networks. https://www.history.com/topics/ancient-rome/colosseum

History.com Editors. (2018, August 21). *Roman Forum*. HISTORY; A&E television networks. https://www.history.com/topics/ancient-rome/roman-forum

Holmes, E. (n.d.). *10 things not to do in Pompeii with kids*. Explore with Erin. https://explorewitherin.com/10-things-not-to-do-in-pompeii-with-kids/

Hot air balloon: where to fly in Tuscany. (2021, May 26). BE BOHEME . https://www.beboheme.com/en/2021/05/26/hot-air-balloon-where-to-fly-in-tuscany/

House of the Faun. (n.d.). Pompeii Sites. http://pompeiisites.org/en/archaeological-site/house-of-the-faun/

House of the Tragic Poet. (n.d.). Pompeii Sites. http://pompeiisites.org/en/archaeological-site/house-of-the-tragic-poet/

House of the Tragic Poet, Pompei. (n.d.). GPSmyCity. https://www.gpsmycity.com/attractions/house-of-the-tragic-poet-27137.html

House of the Vettii. (n.d.). Pompeii Sites. http://pompeiisites.org/en/archaeological-site/house-of-the-vettii/

How to go to Vesuvius: 5 ways to reach the Naples volcano. (n.d.). Visitnaples.eu. https://www.visitnaples.eu/en/neapolitanity/walk-naples/how-to-go-to-vesuvius-5-ways-to-reach-this-volcano-and-some-tips

How to visit Mount Etna? (n.d.). Go-Etna. https://www.go-etna.com/how-to-visit-etna/

I Heart Italy. (2023, January 23). *The best things to do in lucca italy - the famous walled city in Tuscany*. https://iheartitaly.co/things-to-do-in-lucca-italy/

I Heart Italy. (2023, February 3). *The ultimate guide to Sicily*. https://iheartitaly.co/the-ultimate-guide-to-sicily/

I Heart Italy. (2023, February 19). *25 unforgettable things to do in Tuscany*. https://iheartitaly.co/things-to-do-in-tuscany/

Iannone, S. A. (2018, January). *The breathtaking Terrace of Infinity in Villa Cimbrone, Ravello*. Itinari. https://www.itinari.com/the-breathtaking-terrace-of-infinity-in-villa-cimbrone-ravello-8a0a

IICII_Communications. (2020, November 27). *11 interesting facts about Naples that you ought to know*. The Indo Italian Chamber of Commerce and Industry. https://www.indiaitaly.com/post/11-interesting-facts-about-naples-that-you-ought-to-know

Il Vallone delle Ferriere. (n.d.). Www. https://www.positano.com/en/e/il-vallone-delle-ferriere

Imboden, D. (n.d.). *Venice's ghetto*. Venice for Visitors. https://europeforvisitors.com/venice/articles/venice_ghetto.htm

Indro Montanelli Gardens. (n.d.). Italia.it. https://www.italia.it/en/lombardy/milan/mountain-indro-gardens

Is Milan Safe. (2022, December 31). Urban Abroad. https://www.urbanabroad.com/is-milan-safe/

Is Naples safe to visit? (n.d.). This Way to Italy. https://thiswaytoitaly.com/is-naples-safe-to-visit/

Iseo. (n.d.). Lago Iseo. https://visitlakeiseo.info/en/places/iseo/

Island of Murano. (n.d.). Italia.it. https://www.italia.it/en/veneto/venice/venice-island-murano

Italy. (n.d.). UNESCO World Heritage Centre. https://whc.unesco.org/en/statesparties/it

Italy major lakes facts. (n.d.). Interesting Italy Facts. http://www.interesting-italy-facts.com/Italy-Geography-Facts/Interesting-Italy-Lakes-Facts.html

Italy visa and entry requirements. (n.d.). Schengen Visa Info. https://www.schengenvisainfo.com/italy/visa/

Italy, U. (2022, October 25). *How to visit Pompeii on a day trip from Rome*. https://untolditaly.com/pompeii-day-trip-from-rome/#Best_guided_Pompeii_tours_from_rome

ItalySights. (2019, March 28). *Thermal baths in Pompeii - overview of ancient baths*. Italy Sights. https://italy-sights.info/baths_pompeii

Jackie. (2023, April 11). *Churches in Italy: what to wear and other rules*. Jam Travel Tips. https://jamtraveltips.com/europe/churches-in-italy-what-to-wear-and-other-rules/

Jennings, A. (2020, August 17). *Is Italy safe? 5 essential travel tips for visitors*. World Nomads. https://www.worldnomads.com/travel-safety/europe/italy/4-things-to-know-before-going-to-italy

Jeremy. (2023, January 12). *6 tips and traps to avoid while driving in Tuscany*. Living the Dream. https://www.livingthedreamrtw.com/driving-in-tuscany

Jhawar, M. (n.d.). *Booking hotels in Italy: 10 tips*. Italy beyond the Obvious. Retrieved June 19, 2023, from https://italybeyondtheobvious.com/tips-on-booking-hotels-in-italy/

Johnston, D. (2023, May 14). *How to buy tickets to Pompeii in Italy*. Road Affair. https://www.roadaffair.com/buy-tickets-to-pompeii/

Jones, A. (2018, November 23). *A quick guide to Neapolitan pastry*. ItaliaRail. https://www.italiarail.com/food/delight-neapolitan-pastries

Jones, A. (2020, February 17). *When is the best time to visit Italy?* ItaliaRail. https://www.italiarail.com/planning/right-region-right-time-weather-and-tourist-seasons-italy

Julie. (2023, June 9). *15 best things to do on the Amalfi Coast of Italy*. Earth Trekkers. https://www.earthtrekkers.com/best-things-to-do-on-the-amalfi-coast/#2_Take_a_Boat_Tour_of_the_Amalfi_Coast

Julie. (2023, June 9). *Where to stay on the Amalfi Coast in 2023: best hotels & locations*. Earth Trekkers. https://www.earthtrekkers.com/where-to-stay-on-the-amalfi-coast/#Sorrento

Julie. (2023, June 25). *Best way to get around the Amalfi Coast: car, bus, boat, or tour*. Earth Trekkers. https://www.earthtrekkers.com/best-way-to-get-around-the-amalfi-coast/

Julie. (2023, July 1). *Volterra, Italy: best things to do, map, & helpful tips*. Earth Trekkers. https://www.earthtrekkers.com/best-things-to-do-in-volterra-italy/

Jurga. (2023, June 14). *18 must-see places & top things to do in Venice, Italy (+maps & tips)*. Full Suitcase. https://fullsuitcase.com/venice-best-things-to-do/

Karsten, A. (n.d.). *Things to know before renting a car in Italy*. Anna Everywhere. https://annaeverywhere.com/renting-a-car-in-italy/

La Scala Opera House. (n.d.). Summer in Italy. https://www.summerinitaly.com/guide/la-scala-opera-house

Lake Como. (n.d.). Italia.it. https://www.italia.it/en/lombardy/lake-como

Lake Garda. (n.d.). Italia.it. https://www.italia.it/en/italy/lake-garda

Lake Maggiore. (2022, September 26). Italia.it. https://www.italia.it/en/italy/lake-maggiore-villages-islands-castles

Lev-Tov, D. (2022, September 19). *What is Neapolitan pizza?* The Spruce Eats. https://www.thespruceeats.com/what-is-neapolitan-pizza-2708762

Living "la dolce vita": meaning and translation. (n.d.). Think in Italian. https://www.thinkinitalian.com/la-dolce-vita-meaning/

Lucas, G. (Director). (2002). *Star Wars: episode II - attack of the clones* [Film]. 20th Century Fox.

Lucy. (n.d.). *21 do's and don'ts in Italy to avoid the most popular travel mistakes*. Italia like a Local. https://www.italialikealocal.com/21-do-s-and-don-ts-in-italy/#Don%E2%80%99t_expect_public_transportation_to_be_on_time

Lupanar. (n.d.). Pompeii Sites. http://pompeiisites.org/en/archaeological-site/lupanar/

Magi, C. (2022, July 5). *An insider's guide to Sicily: beaches edition*. Sicily Insider. https://sicilyinsider.com/beaches-sicily-guide/

Mallia, E. (n.d.). *Where to stay in Lake Garda*. Miss Tourist. https://misstourist.com/where-to-stay-in-lake-garda-italy/

Manarola. (n.d.). Italian-Riviera.com. https://italian-riviera.com/en/cinque-terre/manarola

Manarola. (n.d.). Italia.it. https://www.italia.it/en/liguria/la-spezia/manarola

Manarola. (n.d.). CinqueTerre.eu.com. https://www.cinqueterre.eu.com/en/manarola

Manarola illuminated nativity scene - Cinque Terre. (n.d.). Italy by Events. https://www.italybyevents.com/en/events/liguria/manarola-nativity-scene/

Masotti, F. (2017, August 15). *13 things tourists should never do in Florence*. Culture Trip. https://theculturetrip.com/europe/italy/articles/13-things-tourists-should-never-do-in-florence/

Masotti, F. (2022, December 7). *Best reasons to visit Siena, Italy*. Culture Trip. https://theculturetrip.com/europe/italy/articles/10-reasons-to-visit-siena-italy/

Mayes, F. (1996). *Under the Tuscan sun: at home in Italy*. Random House.

Medical emergencies while in Italy. (n.d.). U.S. Embassy & Consulates in Italy. https://it.usembassy.gov/u-s-citizen-services/doctors/emergencies/

Monaco, R. (n.d.). *All that you need to know about boat trips in Cinque Terre*. BeautifuLiguria. https://beautifuliguria.com/boat-trips-cinque-terre/

Monreale, Sicily: travel guide for Monreale town and cathedral. (n.d.). Italy This Way. https://www.italythisway.com/places/monreale.php

Monterosso al Mare. (n.d.). Best of Cinque Terre.com. https://www.bestofcinqueterre.com/en/monterosso-al-mare

Monterosso al Mare. (n.d.). Italia.it. https://www.italia.it/en/liguria/la-spezia/monterosso-al-mare

Monterosso: what to see, what to do, where to sleep. (n.d.). Italian-Riviera.com. Retrieved June 26, 2023, from https://italian-riviera.com/en/cinque-terre/monterosso/

Mount Etna. (2022, September 26). Italia.it. https://www.italia.it/en/sicily/catania/things-to-do/mount-etna

Multi-Day tours of the Amalfi Coast. (n.d.). Positano.com. https://www.positano.com/en/e/multi-day-tour-of-the-amalfi-coast

Museum of science and technology with Leonardo. (n.d.). Italia.it. https://www.italia.it/en/lombardy/milan/leonardo-da-vinci-3d-museum-italy

Museum of the Last Supper. (n.d.). Italia.it. https://www.italia.it/en/lombardy/milan/da-vinci-last-supper-museum

Naples Cathedral. (n.d.). Civitatis Naples. https://www.introducingnaples.com/cathedral

Naples National Archaeological Museum. (n.d.). Italia.it. https://www.italia.it/en/campania/naples/national-archaeological-museum-naples

Naples: boat tours, an unmissable experience. (n.d.). Visititaly.eu. https://www.visititaly.eu/places-and-tours/naples-boat-tours-an-unmissable-experience

Nast, C. (2023, May 14). *Lake Orta: an insider's guide to the delights of Italy's most underrated lake*. Condé Nast Traveller. https://www.cntraveller.com/article/lake-orta

Natalie. (2017, December 22). *Best Italian proverbs*. An American in Rome. https://anamericaninrome.com/2017/12/best-italian-proverbs/

Natalie. (2019, May 7). *The splendid Santa Chiara Monastery in Naples*. An American in Rome. https://anamericaninrome.com/2019/05/santa-chiara-naples/

Navigli. (n.d.). Italia.it. https://www.italia.it/en/lombardy/milan/the-navigli

Navona Square. (n.d.). Roma. https://www.turismoroma.it/en/places/navona-square

Nessun Dorma in Manarola – Cinque Terre. (n.d.). CinqueTerre.eu.com. https://www.cinqueterre.eu.com/en/nessun-dorma-cinque-terre

Newman, A. P. (2018, July 19). *Temple of Segesta* (Collector of Experiences, Ed.). Atlas Obscura. https://www.atlasobscura.com/places/temple-of-segesta

Nicky. (n.d.). *Italy travel tips: Do's and don'ts in Italy!* That Anxious Traveler. https://thatanxioustraveller.com/italy-travel-tips-dos-and-donts-in-italy/

Nico. (2023, March 3). *Is Palermo worth it or not?* We Are Palermo. https://wearepalermo.com/news/is-palermo-worth-it/

Northern Sicily's seven volcanic Aeolian Islands. (2022, September 26). Italia.it. https://www.italia.it/en/sicily/things-to-do/aeolians-islands-volcanic-islands

Ormina Tours. (2022, April 4). *7 must see gardens and villas in the lakes region*. https://www.orminatours.com/7-mustsee-gardensvillas/

Pahamotang, E. G. (2021, March 15). *The four seasons of italy and what they offer*. ItalianNotebook. https://www.italiannotebook.com/places/the-four-seasons-of-italy-and-what-they-offer/

Palazzo Contarini del Bovolo. (n.d.). Italia.it. https://www.italia.it/en/veneto/venice/scala-contarini-del-bovolo

Palermo. (n.d.). Visit Sicily. https://www.visitsicily.info/en/localita/palermo/

Pantheon. (n.d.). Italia.it. https://www.italia.it/en/lazio/rome/pantheon

Parco Sempione. (n.d.). Italia.it. https://www.italia.it/en/lombardy/milan/parco-sempione

Parisi, A. (2016, September 13). *Travel itineraries: along the salt road, between Marsala and Trapani*. Sicilians Creativi. https://www.sicilianicreativiincucina.it/itinerari-di-viaggio-lungo-la-via-del-sale-tra-marsala-e-trapani/?lang=en

Phil and Izzy. (n.d.). *Segesta Sicily: absolutely everything you need to know*. The Gap Decaders. https://thegapdecaders.com/visit-segesta/

Piazza del Plebiscito. (n.d.). Civitatis Napples. https://www.introducingnaples.com/piazza-plebiscito

Piazza di Spagna. (n.d.). Italia.it. https://www.italia.it/en/lazio/rome/piazza-di-spagna

Piazza di Spagna & the Spanish Steps. (n.d.). Civitatis Rome. Retrieved July 7, 2023, from https://www.rome.net/piazza-di-spagna?_gl=1

Piazza Navona. (n.d.). Civitatis Rome. https://www.rome.net/piazza-navona

Pinacoteca di Brera. (n.d.). Italia.it. https://www.italia.it/en/lombardy/milan/pinacoteca-di-brera

Pinocchio in Tuscany. (n.d.). Visittuscany.com. https://www.visittuscany.com/en/ideas/pinocchio-in-tuscany/

Pisa. (n.d.). Visittuscany.com. https://www.visittuscany.com/en/destinations/pisa/

Poliero, L. (n.d.). *Piazza del Plebiscito: history and beauty of a historic square in Naples | visitnaples.eu*. Visitnaples.eu. https://www.visitnaples.eu/en/neapolitanity/discover-naples/piazza-del-plebiscito-history-and-beauty-of-a-historic-square-in-naples

Pompeii. (n.d.). Italia.it. https://www.italia.it/en/campania/pompeii-archaeological-site

Pompeii Forum – the main square of the ancient city Pompeii. (2009). Mediterranean Cruise Ports Easy. http://www.mediterranean-cruise-ports-easy.com/pompeii-forum.html

Pompeii vs Herculaneum – what's the difference? (n.d.). Sightseeing Tours Italy. https://www.pompeiitours.it/blog/pompeii-vs-herculaneum-whats-the-difference/

Pompi Online. (2022, March 15). *Pompeii Amphitheatre*. https://www.pompeionline.net/en/archaeological-park-of-pompeii/pompeii-amphitheatre

Ponte dell'Accademia. (n.d.). Venice Travel Guide. Retrieved June 28, 2023, from https://www.venice-travel-guide.com/tourist-attractions/bridges/ponte-dell-accademia

Positano. (n.d.). Italia.it. https://www.italia.it/en/campania/salerno/positano

Pratt, S. E. (2016, March 15). *Benchmarks: March 17, 1944: The most recent eruption of Mount Vesuvius*. Earth. https://www.earthmagazine.org/article/benchmarks-march-17-1944-most-recent-eruption-mount-vesuvius

Prepare your visit. (n.d.). Teatro La Fenice. https://www.teatrolafenice.it/en/prepare-your-visit/

Pucciarelli, E. (2016, July 18). *28 famous movies set in Tuscany*. My Travel in Tuscany. https://mytravelintuscany.com/25-movies-set-in-tuscany/

Quadrilatero della moda. (n.d.). Italia.it. https://www.italia.it/en/lombardy/milan/milan-fashion-district

Ravello. (n.d.). Italia.it. https://www.italia.it/en/campania/salerno/ravello

Ravello - Italy. (n.d.). Positano.com. https://www.positano.com/en/e/ravello

Rhonda. (2013, January 20). *Watersports on the Italian Lakes*. Unstoppable Family. https://unstoppablefamily.com/watersports-on-the-italian-lakes/

Rialto Bridge. (n.d.). Italia.it. https://www.italia.it/en/veneto/venice/rialto-bridge

Rialto Market, Venice: a must visit. (n.d.). NextStop-Italy. https://nextstop-italy.com/food-drink/venices-markets-spritz-boat/

Riomaggiore. (n.d.). Italian-Riviera.com. https://italian-riviera.com/en/cinque-terre/riomaggiore

Riomaggiore. (n.d.). CinqueTerre.eu.com. https://www.cinqueterre.eu.com/en/riomaggiore

Roman Forum and Palatine Hill. (n.d.). Siti Archeologici D'Italia. https://www.sitiarcheologiciditalia.it/en/roman-forum-and-palatine-hill/

Rome food and cuisine. (n.d.). Rome.info. https://www.rome.info/food/

Rome Guide. (n.d.). *A guide to the Trevi Fountain: everything you need to know*. Roma Experience. https://www.romaexperience.com/post/trevi-fountain

Rome in a nutshell. (n.d.). Roma. https://www.turismoroma.it/en/page/rome-nutshell

Rosemary. (2022, March 22). *9 of the best Etna wineries to visit in Sicily for amazing Etna wines*. Authentic Food Quest. https://www.authenticfoodquest.com/best-mount-etna-wineries-sicily-wines/

Rough Guides Editors. (2023, April 16). *Unforgettable things to do in Tuscany*. Rough Guides. https://www.roughguides.com/articles/unforgettable-things-to-do-tuscany-italy

Royal Palace in Naples. (n.d.). Italia.it. https://www.italia.it/en/campania/naples/royal-palace-naples

Ruffa, G. (2023, May 2). *Italian dining etiquette: do's and don'ts*. The Italy Edit. https://www.theitalyedit.com/italian-etiquette-dos-donts/

Sabino, C. (2019, May 12). *5 amazing Italian Lake towns you really shouldn't miss*. Forbes. https://www.forbes.com/sites/catherinesabino/2019/05/12/5-amazing-italian-lake-towns-you-really-shouldnt-miss/?sh=73d12fc13c6b

Sailing and boating in Italy. (n.d.). Angloinfo. https://www.angloinfo.com/how-to/italy/lifestyle/sports-leisure/sailing

Salerno. (n.d.). Italia.it. https://www.italia.it/en/campania/salerno

San Gimignano – the medieval town of Tuscany, Italy. (n.d.). Love from Tuscany. https://lovefromtuscany.com/where-to-go/small-towns-in-tuscany/san-gimignano-what-to-see-and-do/

San Maurizio al Monastero Maggiore. (n.d.). Civitatis Milan. https://www.introducingmilan.com/san-maurizio-al-monastero-maggiore

San Siro Stadium. (n.d.). Italia.it. https://www.italia.it/en/lombardy/milan/meazza-san-siro-stadium

Scala Contarini del Bovolo. (n.d.). Atlas Obscura. Retrieved June 28, 2023, from https://www.atlasobscura.com/places/scala-contarini-del-bovolo

Searle, A. J. (2021, October 28). *Where to hike around Italy's great lakes*. The Italy Edit. https://www.theitalyedit.com/hiking-italian-lakes/

See the best of Arezzo. (n.d.). Love from Tuscany. https://lovefromtuscany.com/where-to-go/cities-in-tuscany/arezzo/

Selinunte. (n.d.). Siti Archeologici D'Italia. https://www.sitiarcheologiciditalia.it/en/archaeological-park-selinunte/

7 reasons to take a cooking class in Tuscany, Italy. (2023, May 11). Travel for Food Hub. https://travelforfoodhub.com/cooking-class-in-tuscany-italy/

7 tips for commuting in Italy by bus or train. (n.d.). Italy Now. https://italynow.com/blog/7-tips-commuting-in-italy-bus-or-train/

17 must know tips for driving in Italy. (n.d.). Adventurous Kate. https://www.adventurouskate.com/driving-in-italy/

Sforzesco Castle. (n.d.). Italia.it. Retrieved June 23, 2023, from https://www.italia.it/en/lombardy/milan/castello-sforzesco

Sicily food guide: the flavors of Sicilian cuisine and what to eat there. (n.d.). Italy Foodies. https://www.italyfoodies.com/blog/sicily-food-sicilian-cuisine-what-to-eat-in-sicily

Sicily's best beaches. (n.d.). Frommer's. https://www.frommers.com/slideshows/818840-sicily-s-best-beaches

Siggers, R. (2020, June 24). *Six mistakes to avoid when planning a trip to Italy*. Clio Muse Tours. https://cliomusetours.com/six-mistakes-to-avoid-when-planning-a-trip-to-italy/

Sistine Chapel. (n.d.-a). Civitatis Rome. https://www.rome.net/sistine-chapel?_gl=1

Sistine Chapel. (n.d.). Italia.it. https://www.italia.it/en/lazio/rome/cappella-sistina

Sistine Chapel. (n.d.). Rome.info. https://www.rome.info/attractions/sistine-chapel/

Sonnet. (n.d.). The Spiritual Life. https://slife.org/sonnet/

Spaccanapoli. (n.d.). Naples Italy. https://naplesitaly.it/spaccanapoli/

Spaccanapoli. (n.d.). Civitatis Naples. https://www.introducingnaples.com/spaccanapoli

St. Mark square. (n.d.). Italia.it. https://www.italia.it/en/veneto/venice/st-marks-square

St. Peter's Basilica. (n.d.). Civitatis Rome. https://www.rome.net/st-peters-basilica?_gl=1

Steph. (2020, February 5). *A foodie's guide to the Cinque Terre*. The Mediterranean Traveller. https://www.themediterraneantraveller.com/cinque-terre-food/

Syracuse. (n.d.). Italia.it. https://www.italia.it/en/sicily/siracusa

Syracuse. (n.d.). Visit Sicily. https://www.visitsicily.info/en/localita/siracusa/

Taborda, J. (2023, February 23). *Climate and seasons of Italy*. Expatica Italy. https://www.expatica.com/it/moving/about/climate-and-seasons-in-italy-79363

Take a stroll through fashion: a short guide to the most beautiful Milan fashion week locations. (n.d.). Italia.it. Retrieved June 26, 2023, from https://www.italia.it/en/lombardy/milan/things-to-do/best-locations-where-milan-fashion-week-is-held

Taormina, a natural platform overlooking the sea. (2022, July 20). Italia.it. https://www.italia.it/en/sicily/taormina/guide-history-facts

Tarot Garden. (n.d.). Visittuscany.com. https://www.visittuscany.com/en/attractions/tarot-garden/

Team Acko. (2022, December 13). *Best time and season to visit Italy: complete guide*. Acko. https://www.acko.com/travel-tips/best-time-to-visit-italy/

Team, E. (2023, March 22). *Best trattorias in Milan*. The Italian Escape. https://www.theitalianescape.com/milan/food/best-trattorias-in-milan/

Teatro alla Scala. (n.d.). Italia.it. https://www.italia.it/en/lombardy/milan/milan-opera-house-la-scala

Teatro dell'Opera – Rome Opera House. (n.d.). Roma. https://turismoroma.it/en/places/teatro-dell%E2%80%99opera-rome-opera-house

Teatro di San Carlo. (n.d.). Civitatis Naples. https://www.introducingnaples.com/teatro-san-carlo

Temple of Apollo. (n.d.). Sightseeing Tours Italy. https://www.sightseeingtoursitaly.com/attractions/temple-of-apollo/

10 best Chianti towns to visit. (n.d.). Love from Tuscany. https://lovefromtuscany.com/10-best-towns-visit-in-chianti/

10 don'ts in Rome – our little survival guide. (n.d.). Tourist in Rom. https://www.tourist-in-rom.com/en/donts-in-rome/

10 lakes in Italy for an active holiday. (2022, July 19). Italia.it. https://www.italia.it/en/italy/things-to-do/10-lakes-in-italy-for-an-active-holiday

10 mistakes people make when visiting milan. (n.d.). Hotels.com. https://ph.hotels.com/go/italy/mistakes-people-make-when-visiting-milan

10 most famous Roman dishes. (n.d.). Italy Best. https://italybest.com/10-most-famous-roman-dishes-to-eat-in-rome-italy/

Ten things not to do on your Sicilian Trip. (n.d.). Streaty.com. https://www.streaty.com/blog/ten-things-not-to-do-in-sicily

The Bacaro tour: a Venetian tradition. (n.d.). Visitvenezia.eu. https://www.visitvenezia.eu/en/venetianity/walk-venice/the-bacaro-tour-a-venetian-tradition

The best tour companies in Italy. (2022, January 24). Nomadic Matt. https://www.nomadicmatt.com/travel-blogs/best-tour-companies-italy/

The Blue Path. (n.d.). Italia.it. https://www.italia.it/en/liguria/la-spezia/sentiero-azzurro

The Bridge of Sighs. (n.d.). Venezia Autentica. https://veneziaautentica.com/bridge-of-sighs-in-venice/

The Casts. (n.d.). Pompeii Sites. http://pompeiisites.org/en/pompeii-map/analysis/the-casts/

The Catacombs of Naples. (2022, July 18). Italia.it. https://www.italia.it/en/campania/naples/things-to-do/naples-catacombs

The cats of Rome. (n.d.). AESU. https://www.aesu.com/italy-travel-tips/the-cats-of-rome/

The Emerald Grotto (Grotta dello Smeraldo) in Amalfi. (n.d.). Positano.com. https://www.positano.com/en/e/visiting-the-emerald-grotto-amalfi

The Go Ahead Tours Team. (2021, September 10). *Must-see works of Renaissance art in Florence*. Go Ahead Tours. https://www.goaheadtours.com/travel-blog/articles/must-see-art-in-florence

The Great Salt Road, Sicily. (n.d.). NextStop-Italy. Retrieved July 14, 2023, from https://nextstop-italy.com/inspire/salt-windmills-flamingos/

The history of the word "ciao" & why you shouldn't say it in Italy. (n.d.). ItalyExplained. https://italyexplained.com/the-history-of-the-word-ciao-why-you-shouldnt-say-it-in-italy/

The House of Vettii in historic context. (n.d.). MIT. https://web.mit.edu/course/21/21h.405/www/vettii/sources.html

The Lupanar. (n.d.). PlanetPompeii. https://www.planetpompeii.com/en/map/the-lupanar.html

The National Archaeological Museum of Naples: the ancient lighthouse. (n.d.). Visitnaples.eu. https://www.visitnaples.eu/en/neapolitanity/discover-naples/the-national-archaeological-museum-of-naples-the-ancient-lighthouse

The nine best neighborhoods to stay in Milan. (n.d.). Italy4Real. https://italy4real.com/best-neighborhoods-in-milan/

The Opera Theater of Rome. (n.d.). Italia.it. https://www.italia.it/en/lazio/rome/teatro-dell-opera-rome

The Pantheon. (n.d.). Roma. https://www.turismoroma.it/en/places/pantheon

The Spanish Steps in Rome. (n.d.). RomeSite.com. https://romesite.com/spanish-steps.html

The Valley of the Temples in Agrigento, an archaeological wonder in a dream setting. (n.d.). Italia.it. Retrieved September 20, 202 C.E., from https://www.italia.it/en/sicily/agrigento/things-to-do/agrigento-valley-of-the-temples

The Villa Romana del Casale in Piazza Armerina. (2022, September 26). Italia.it. https://www.italia.it/en/sicily/things-to-do/villa-romana-del-casale

Things to do and see in the Cinque Terre. (n.d.). CinqueTerre.eu.com. https://www.cinqueterre.eu.com/en/cinque-terre-what-to-do-see

3 wine destinations in Tuscany. (n.d.). Visittuscany.com. Retrieved July 5, 2023, from https://www.visittuscany.com/en/itineraries/3-places-drink-wine-tuscany/

Tiber River. (n.d.). Italia.it. https://www.italia.it/en/lazio/rome/river-tevere

Tickets. (n.d.). Duomo Di Milano. https://ticket.duomomilano.it/en/biglietti/

Torcello. (n.d.). Atlas Obscura. https://www.atlasobscura.com/places/torcello

Tourist seasons in Italy: high, low, & shoulders. (n.d.). Italy Explained. https://italyexplained.com/tourist-seasons-in-italy-high-low-shoulders/

Trastevere. (n.d.). Civitatis Rome. https://www.rome.net/trastevere

Trastevere, Rome. (n.d.). RomeSite.com. https://romesite.com/trastevere.html

Travel insurance for Italy – health insurance guide for tourists in Italy. (n.d.). SchengenVisainfo. https://www.schengenvisainfo.com/europe-travel-insurance/italy/

Travel insurance: USA to Italy trip. (2023, June 10). Forbes Advisor. https://www.forbes.com/advisor/travel-insurance/destinations/italy-trips/

Travel safety in Italy: tourist scams to watch for. (n.d.). Italy Explained. https://italyexplained.com/travel-safety-in-italy-tourist-scams-to-watch-for/

Turansky, M. (2023, April 10). *8 best towns to stay in Lake Como, Italy*. The World Was Here First. https://www.theworldwasherefirst.com/best-town-to-stay-in-lake-como/

Turtle, M. (2023, May 9). *Pompeii: frozen in time*. Time Travel Turtle. https://www.timetravelturtle.com/visit-pompeii-self-guided-tour-italy/

Tuscany. (n.d.). Italia.it. https://www.italia.it/en/tuscany

12 interesting facts about Rome. (n.d.). WorldStrides. https://worldstrides.com/blog/2016/10/12-interesting-facts-about-rome/

2022 global peace index. (2022). Vision of Humanity. https://www.visionofhumanity.org/maps/#/

Untold Italy. (2021, December 22). *How to choose the best time to visit Italy*. https://untolditaly.com/the-best-time-to-visit-italy/

Untold Italy. (2022, April 22). *Episode #120: mistakes to avoid when planning your trip to Italy*. https://untolditaly.com/episode-120-mistakes-to-avoid-when-planning-your-trip-to-italy/

Untold Italy. (2022, September 21). *What is the best area to stay in Rome?* https://untolditaly.com/best-place-to-stay-in-rome/

Val d'Orcia. (n.d.). Italia.it. https://www.italia.it/en/tuscany/siena/val-d-orcia

Valle delle Ferriere. (n.d.). Live Salerno. https://www.livesalerno.com/valle-delle-ferriere

Veidehi. (2023, July 7). *9 best things to do in Pompeii, Italy – updated 2023*. Trip101. https://trip101.com/article/things-to-do-pompeii

Venetian mask making workshop in Venice. (n.d.). Klook Travel. https://www.klook.com/en-SG/activity/16611-venetian-mask-making-workshop-venice/

Venice ghetto glass. (n.d.). Italia.it. https://www.italia.it/en/veneto/venice/jewish-ghetto-venice

Vernazza. (n.d.). Italian-Riviera.com. https://italian-riviera.com/en/cinque-terre/vernazza

Vernazza. (n.d.). Italia.it. https://www.italia.it/en/liguria/la-spezia/vernazza

Vernazza. (n.d.). CinqueTerre.eu.com. https://www.cinqueterre.eu.com/en/vernazza

Via del Corso. (n.d.). Italia.it. https://www.italia.it/en/lazio/rome/via-del-corso

Via del Corso. (n.d.). Roma. https://www.turismoroma.it/en/places/via-del-corso

Villa Necchi Campiglio. (n.d.). Italia.it. https://www.italia.it/en/lombardia/milano/museums/villa-campiglio

Villa of the Mysteries. (n.d.). Pompeii Sites. http://pompeiisites.org/en/archaeological-site/villa-of-the-mysteries/

Villa Romana del Casale. (n.d.). Italia.it. https://www.italia.it/en/sicily/enna/villa-romana-del-casale

Visa for Italy. (n.d.). Farnesina. https://vistoperitalia.esteri.it/home.aspx#BMQuestionario

Visit Florence, Italy – travel guide. (n.d.). FlorenceTips.com. https://florencetips.com/

Volterra. (n.d.). Visittuscany.com. https://www.visittuscany.com/en/destinations/volterra/

Walker, A. (2023, June 13). *Public transportation in Italy.* Expatica Italy. https://www.expatica.com/it/living/transportation/public-transportation-italy-80076/#coaches

Wang, I. (2022, December 30). *Things tourists should never do in Venice, Italy.* Culture Trip. https://theculturetrip.com/europe/italy/articles/13-things-tourists-should-never-do-in-venice-italy/

Weitz, C. (Director). (2009). *The Twilight Saga: New Moon* [Film]. Summit Entertainment.

Wells, A. (Director). (2003). Under the Tuscan Sun [Film]. Touchstone.

What to pack for a trip to Italy. (n.d.). Italofile. https://www.italofile.com/what-to-pack-italy/

What to see in Milan. (n.d.). Italia.it. https://www.italia.it/en/lombardy/milan

Where to stay in Milan: tips from a local. (2023, February 2). Greta's Travels. https://gretastravels.com/where-to-stay-in-milan/#Best_areas_to_stay_in_Milan_at_a_glance

Where to stay in Naples: 9 best areas. (n.d.). The Nomadvisor. https://thenomadvisor.com/where-to-stay-in-naples/

Where to stay in Sicily: 14 best areas. (n.d.). The Nomadvisor. https://thenomadvisor.com/where-to-stay-in-sicily/

Where to stay in Venice: 8 best areas. (2022, January 9). The Nomadvisor. https://thenomadvisor.com/where-to-stay-in-venice/

Where to stay on Lago Maggiore: the towns of Italy's most beautiful lakes. (2022, March 11). Through Eternity Tours. https://www.througheternity.com/en/blog/travel-tips/where-to-stay-lake-maggiore.html

Why go to Amalfi Coast. (n.d.). U.S. News. https://travel.usnews.com/Amalfi_Coast_Italy/

Winick, G. (Director). (2010). *Letters to Juliet* [Film]. Summit Entertainment.

Wolters, M. (2022, December 8). *What not to do when visiting Pompeii.* Wolters World. https://woltersworld.com/what-not-to-do-when-visiting-pompeii/

Wood, M. (2019, September 4). *11 rookie mistakes to avoid in Cinque Terre.* Oyster. https://www.oyster.com/articles/mistakes-to-avoid-in-cinque-terre/

Zemeckis, R. (Director). (2022). *Pinocchio* [Film]. Walt Disney Pictures.

Zinna, A. (2023, May 3). *The best time to go to Italy.* Lonely Planet. https://www.lonelyplanet.com/articles/best-time-to-visit-italy

Zucchi, L. (2022, February 25). *10 things not to do in Milan.* Res Humana. https://www.reshumana.com/cities/milan/10-things-not-to-do-in-milan/

Zusman, K. (n.d.). *The Tiber River in Rome.* Rome.us. https://rome.us/ancient-rome/the-tiber-river.html

Image References

IgorSaveliev. (2015). Sforzesco castle, Milan, Italy image [Image]. In *Pixabay.* https://pixabay.com/photos/sforzesco-castle-milan-italy-705898/

Bericchia, M. (2020). Brown concrete building in Val d'Orcia [Image]. In *Unsplash.* https://unsplash.com/photos/fSfgZCofQz0

chatst2. (2017). Stadium, The san siro, Meazza image [Image]. In *Pixabay.* https://pixabay.com/photos/stadium-the-san-siro-meazza-milan-2753288/

Goerend, J. (2020). Italian vineyard landscape during sunset. In Tuscany [Image]. In *Unsplash.* https://unsplash.com/photos/pnigODapPek

Gomez Angel, R. (2018). Venice canal photo [Image]. In *Unsplash.* https://unsplash.com/photos/t2yh3mlISdQ

Hogendoorn, F. (2020). Piazza Navona [Image]. In *Unsplash.* https://unsplash.com/photos/lqobU_InJFI

Kaden, H. (2018a). Sometimes we all need a little shoulder to lean on [Image]. In *Unsplash.* https://unsplash.com/photos/XvPsA9Riev4

Kaden, H. (2018b). Saving the best for last! [Image]. In *Unsplash.* https://unsplash.com/photos/xWZa0GYCMbo

Karvounis, N. (2017). The Bridge of Sighs. In *Unsplash.* https://unsplash.com/photos/EEK-6CvoUr8

Lugaresi, L. (2020). Volterra tuscany italy city colours [Image]. In *Unsplash.* https://unsplash.com/photos/ovKg2NvNQNo

LunarSeaArt. (2017). Venice Rialto Italy [Image]. In *Pixabay.* https://pixabay.com/photos/venice-rialto-italy-bridge-2085864/

Meier, B. (2020). Lake Como, Italy [Image]. In *Unplash.* https://unsplash.com/photos/hOXrXJeE6dQ

Michelle_Maria. (2015). Apartments for rent [Image]. In *Pixabay.* https://pixabay.com/photos/italy-cinque-terre-storefront-1041660/

Mondì , G. (n.d.). Vernazza City sunset photo [Image]. In *Burst.shopify.* https://burst.shopify.com/photos/vernazza-city-sunset?q=vernazza

NakNakNak. (2021). Italy, Venice, St Mark's Square [Image]. In *Pixabay.* https://pixabay.com/photos/italy-venice-st-marks-square-night-6735334/

Peyrard, L. (2021). Cute street in Milan's Navigli neighborhood [Image]. In *Unsplash.* https://unsplash.com/photos/fI0NXDRxcVw

Snelders, B. (2019). Cinque Terre night view [Image]. In *Unsplash.* https://unsplash.com/photos/PeLkhi_B3wI

Takil, A. (2018). Colourful beach umbrellas seen from above [Image]. In *Unsplash.* https://unsplash.com/photos/Q31gya7_kho

vivianamartinelli1979. (2014). Milan, Duomo, monument image [Image]. In *Pixabay.* https://pixabay.com/photos/milan-duomo-monument-italy-273124/

von Bibra, L. (2019). Rooftops of bella Venezia [Image]. In *Unsplash.* https://unsplash.com/photos/4IjOCxtHc6Y

Copyright of rest of the images has bought on depositphotos.com